HERMANUS

WHALES • WINE • FYNBOS • ART

BETH HUNT

Photography by Johann and Kobus Kruger

DEDICATION

For my brother, Jeffrey Tanner,
who loved Hermanus (14.5.1951–29.9.2015)

For Jean-Francois 'Jifa' Avenier – wildlife photographer
whose passion was the great white shark (25.5.1947–21.6.2014)

Published by Struik Travel & Heritage
(an imprint of Penguin Random House South Africa (Pty) Ltd)
Reg. No. 1953/000441/07

The Estuaries No. 4, Oxbow Crescent, Century Avenue, Century City, 7441
PO Box 1144, Cape Town, 8000 South Africa

Visit www.penguinrandomhouse.co.za

First published in 2017
1 3 5 7 9 10 8 6 4 2

Print: 978 1 77584 547 8
ePub: 978 1 77584 563 8
ePDF: 978 1 77584 564 5

Copyright © in text, 2017: Beth Hunt
Copyright © in photographs, 2017: Johann and Kobus Kruger,
and as shown alongside
Copyright © in map, 2017: Peter Earl
Copyright © in published edition, 2017:
Penguin Random House South Africa (Pty) Ltd

Publisher: Pippa Parker
Managing editor: Helen de Villiers
Project manager: Roelien Theron
Editor: Charles de Villiers
Designer: Janice Evans
Proofreader: Thea Grobbelaar

Reproduction by Hirt & Carter Cape (Pty) Ltd
Printed and bound in China by Leo Paper Products Ltd., Hong Kong
All rights reserved. No part of this publication may be reproduced,
stored in a retrieval system, or transmitted, in any form or by any means,
electronic, mechanical, photocopying, recording or otherwise, without
the prior written permission of the copyright owner(s).

All photography © Johann and Kobus Kruger, except for the following:
p. 21: Wikimedia Commons, public domain; p. 22 (l): Painted by Frans Groenewald,
© Kogelberg Biosphere Reserve; pp. 30–43: De Wet's Huis Photographic Museum,
Hermanus; p. 48: Museum Africa; p. 50: Wellcome Library, London; p. 65 (t): Colette
Stott; p. 67: Western Cape Archives and Record Service; pp. 72, 76 (b) & 78: White
Shark Projects; pp. 116 & 125 (r): Old Harbour Museum; p. 143: Colette Stott;
p. 152 (tl): Albert Froneman/Images of Africa; p. 158: Hamilton Russell Vineyards;
p. 159 (t): Micky Hoyle/Images of Africa; p. 161 (t, bl): Bouchard Finlayson;
p. 162: La Vierge; p. 163 (tr, b): Andries Joubert/Newton Johnson;
pp. 192–193: Gabriel Athiros ; p. 196 (l): Maureen Tomaino

Key: t = top, c = centre, b = bottom, l = left, r = right

Front cover: Kayaking near the Old Harbour.
Title page: A paraglider soars above Hermanus.
Pages 2–3: Hermanus village, nestled between the Klein River
Mountains and Walker Bay.
Pages 4–5: The tidal pool at The Marine.
Opposite page: Viewing dolphins up-close in Walker Bay.
Back cover: The Old Harbour.

CONTENTS

Preface 9

Foreword 13

En route 15

An overview 29

People and places 49

The whales of Walker Bay 59

The sharks of Walker Bay 72

The town centre – heart of Hermanus 81

Cultural highlights 95

Hermanus on the map 108

The natural beauty of Hermanus 129

The Hemel-en-Aarde Valley 156

Beyond Hermanus 181

Bibliography 196

Acknowledgements 198

Kayaking close to the cliffs at Bay View.

PREFACE

Set on the cliffs, between the mountains and the sea, in an environment of exceptional beauty lies the fabled whale capital of the world, Hermanus.

It is to this Western Cape shoreline that the southern right whales make their annual migration from Antarctica – a unique attraction that has placed the seaside town on the international tourist map. Visitors come from across the globe to experience a sighting of these magnificent mammals as well as to enjoy the scenic biodiversity, which creates the tapestry of this Overberg landscape at the tip of Africa.

Hermanus, with its Mediterranean climate and seasonal champagne air, is sometimes called the 'Riviera of the South'. It started out in the mid-1800s as a quiet fishing village, built on a rocky escarpment alongside an ocean teeming with marine life. Today it's a different story. The changing tides of time, population growth and progress have turned the town into one of South Africa's most popular tourism hotspots. Rich in natural splendour, Hermanus also attracts those seeking a quality and creative lifestyle.

Right: Panoramic vista of Hermanus, from Westcliff to Voëlklip.

Below: A jogger takes a breather at Sievers Point.

The charm and appeal of Hermanus have not ceased to captivate new settlers since its establishment more than 150 years ago, and the village that once was has since grown into a thriving and vibrant metropolis of the region.

In the past, famous South African writers and artists, such as Jan Rabie, Uys Krige, Marjorie Wallace, Cecil Higgs and Gregoire Boonzaier have made their homes here. The once-controversial South African author Stuart Cloete and his American wife, Tiny, settled on a farm in the area of Stanford near Hermanus. Cloete's first novel, *Turning Wheels*, published in 1937, was banned in South Africa because of its commentary on the Great Trek.

Nowadays, Hermanus residents also include a coterie of homeowners who leave the European winters to spend summers here. They are known as 'swallows' and their numbers make up a substantial 'flock'.

With the start of the winter season, the local residents celebrate the return of the whales to Walker Bay, as well as the arrival of tourists who come to meet and greet these denizens of the deep.

Throughout the year, Hermanus draws weekenders from Cape Town and other surrounding areas to spend a relaxing interlude at this seaside resort, far from the fast tempo of city living and the routine of daily life.

Both Christmas and Easter vacations are peak seasons and a time of year when the town is full to the brim with visitors.

There is no doubt that this locale nestled in the Overberg is high on the list of the most desirable places to visit in South Africa.

Hermanus histories

- In 1889, 500 people lived in a cluster of fishermen's cottages in what was then known as Hermanuspietersfontein.
- A hundred years later, in 1989, approximately 7,500 people inhabited this 12-kilometre crescent (now known as Hermanus) between the mountains and the sea.
- By 1992 the population figure stood at almost 13,000.
- In 2010 the population of Hermanus exceeded 40,000. By 2016 this figure increased to approximately 90,000.
- After Cape Town, Hermanus is reputed to be the fastest-growing town in the Western Cape.

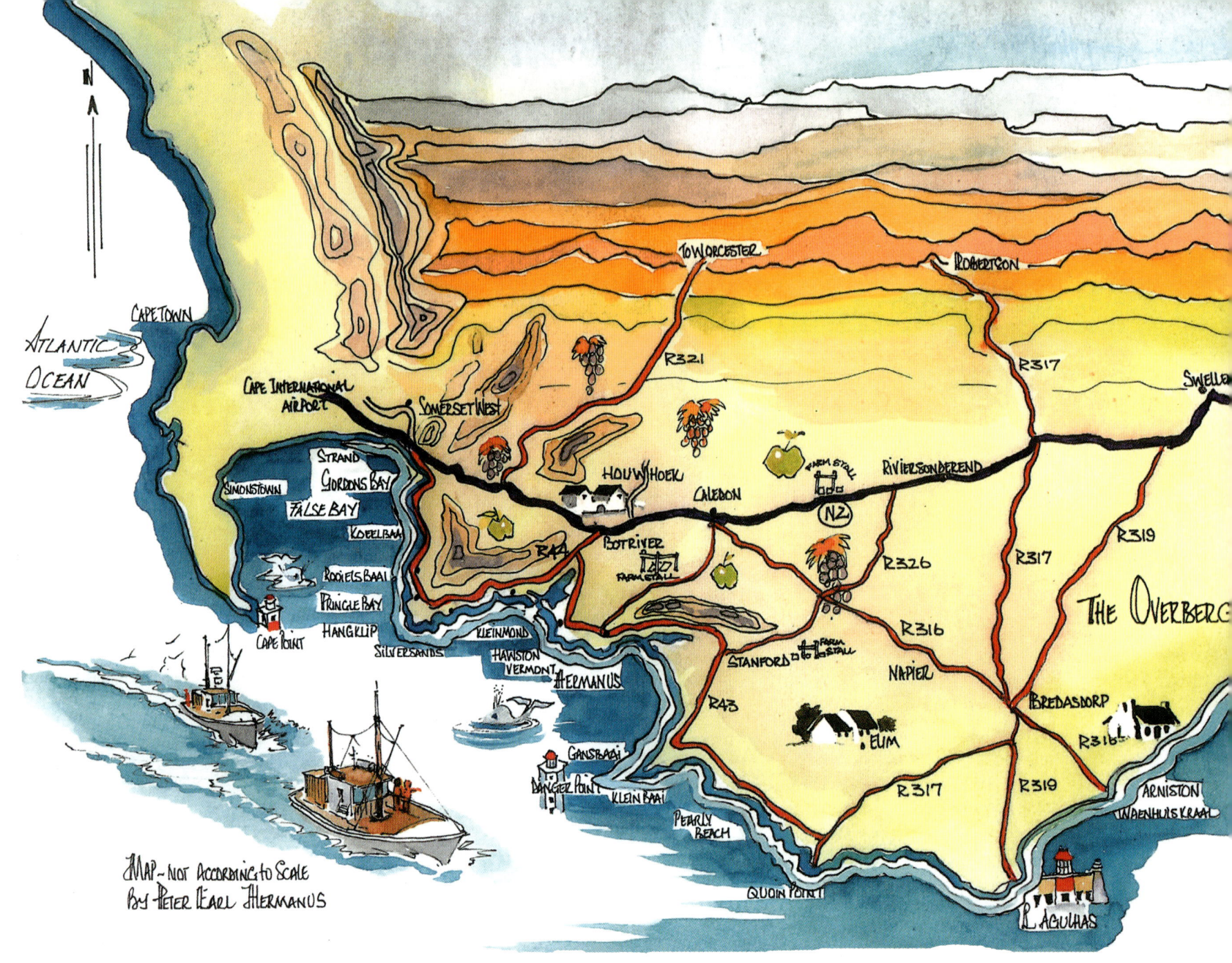

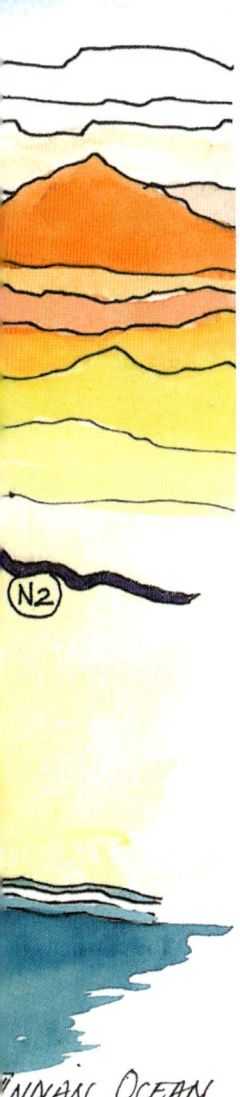

FOREWORD

BY DR ROBIN LEE,
HERMANUS HISTORY SOCIETY

Hermanus is a remarkable place. The most casual of tourists experiences its distinctive flavour, as can be seen in the pleasure and surprise expressed in thousands of comments posted on the websites of hotels, guesthouses, restaurants and organisations offering a variety of tourism experiences. Almost without exception the posts refer to unexpected and pleasurable experiences.

Why should this be the case? After all, Hermanus is a middle-sized town, with a rapidly growing population, an unemployment problem and a large retired population that might be expected to look askance on modernisation.

The answer is celebrated in Beth Hunt's book. In a word: 'diversity' – the diversity of experiences that Hermanus offers and the range of visitors it attracts, without (as yet) one of these dominating all the others. This book does full justice to the diversity of the town and the region, as it covers destinations from Pringle Bay to Danger Point and inland. The town's main attractions – whales, wine, fynbos and art – feature prominently. To these we can add at least a few more: harbours; mountain-bike trails; sharks; scenic walks; golf courses; hotels; markets; and glimpses of history. And, although this may not be consciously experienced by the visitor, Hermanus benefits greatly from the administrative competence of what is almost certainly one of the best municipalities in the country.

The book covers all these aspects in laudable detail and with a fresh eye. The author combines fact with a lyrical feel and offers hints and recommendations, making the book useful as a reference work as well as bedtime reading. I am sure it will find an enthusiastic audience.

Hermanus has so far avoided the fate of many coastal holiday towns, that of becoming so popular that the pressure of numbers destroys the features that made the town popular in the first place. This book offers a wide spectrum of information and insight and gives the reader a clear indication of the aspects of present-day Hermanus that should be regarded as heritage, and preserved. At the same time, it does full justice to modern developments, such as the trend towards ecotourism.

Map of the Overberg.

EN ROUTE

*'It is good to have an end to journey toward;
but it is the journey that matters, in the end.'*

Ernest Hemingway

When travelling by road from Cape Town to Hermanus you have the option of either an inland or a coastal route. The N2 freeway takes you on an inland journey of approximately 90 minutes, crossing Sir Lowry's Pass, named after Sir Galbraith Lowry Cole, a far-sighted Governor of the Cape who braved the displeasure of the British government to construct this essential link. Previously the route had been known as the Elandspad (meaning 'path of the eland'). In 1984 the upper, overhanging four-lane section was built; in its day, it was considered an engineering marvel. This is where the Overberg ('over the mountain') region begins, stretching along the majestic Hottentots Holland mountain range (known to pioneering settlers as the Mountains of Africa). The road makes a steep ascent against the granite slopes before dipping to follow the contour alongside a pine forest framing the large Steenbras Dam, which supplies water to Cape Town.

Running alongside the old Cape Wagon Route, the road stretches into the Grabouw Valley, forested by timber plantations, with its vineyards and fruit orchards, bordered by fences of rambling roses, creating a spectacular seasonal display. Along the way, farm stalls welcome the traveller with local produce and cellar wines. Boutique gift shops and restaurants offer an inviting pause on the journey.

Clarence Drive, hugging the False Bay coastline between Gordon's Bay and Kleinmond, is one of the most scenic routes linking Cape Town and Hermanus.

HERMANUS 15

Also located on the N2 is the oldest coaching inn and licensed hotel in South Africa. The Houw Hoek Hotel, founded in 1834, was originally the site of the tollgate established in the days of the Dutch East India Company. Travel back in time to when the cattle trail, used by the early Cape government officials, passed in front of the clay-walled building. Picture ox wagons drawing up with a clatter of hooves as heavy wooden and brass trunks are unloaded after dusty days of travelling. At that time, this was the only route from Cape Town into the Overberg, and the journey from the Colony by ox wagon took four days. The old post-cart also used to stop at Houw Hoek. In 1900, when the railway line to Caledon was built, the inn became the food depot for the railway.

As ox wagons were replaced by horse-drawn coaches and carts in the early part of the twentieth century, Cape Town judges stayed at Houw Hoek while they conducted Circuit Court sessions in the Overberg region.

Standing sentry outside the hotel's quaint pub is one of the largest blue gum trees in the country; it is approximately 200 years old, and looks as if it has been there forever.

The Houw Hoek Hotel first opened its doors in 1834 as a coaching inn. At its entrance stands one of the largest blue gum trees in the country.

In 1798, Lady Anne Barnard travelled over the Houw Hoek Pass with her husband, the Colonial Secretary, and friends on an exploratory expedition from Cape Town. Lady Anne's journals of her sojourn in Africa are an informative source of South African history, and valuable items of Africana today.

An excerpt from one of her letters reads:

Monday May 7th, 1798

We started at seven o'clock in the morning, the weather glorious, and all our animals well. We had to engage a further team of twelve oxen to carry us over Howe-hook, another tremendous hill. These cattle were so strong that they pulled us with ease up perpendicular ascents, which made me think that they would pull us like Elijah up to heaven. The vegetation, of tender green and olive and brown, was fresher than the day before. The rocks appeared to be of a bastard white marble, but they said they were limestone; and a lot of the most brilliant everlasting flowers, pinked with black hearts, grew among the heath. The descent was two miles, and before us opened a wide desert, pathless, untenanted; one little bit of smoke only ascended to heaven — it looked like the fire offering of Cain. Probably it was the fire of some poor Hottentot cooking his humble mess. We now got on to what is called 'The Great Road', tolerably well beaten by wagons. We were going on to a Mynheer Brandt's where we intended to pass the night; but we stopped halfway at a farmhouse to rest the horses and have something to eat. I was very tired, and I thought the stoep in front of the house the pleasantest of all seats. We made the best meal we could, having as a table the top of an old barrel.

Lady Anne Barnard, *South Africa a Century Ago; Letters Written from the Cape of Good Hope (1797–1801)*, 1910

In 1798, when Lady Anne Barnard and her husband, Andrew Barnard, crossed the Hottentots Holland Mountains, it was along a narrow, treacherous wagon path. Today, the four-lane Sir Lowry's Pass, between Somerset West and the Elgin Valley, effortlessly carries traffic into the once inaccessible interior.

The views from Sir Lowry's Pass over the Overberg and the Helderberg mountain range in the distance are spectacular. Work on the pass started in 1829 and was completed in 1830, making travel between the Cape Colony and the farming districts in the interior faster and safer.

In winter, the Overberg landscape turns to gold as the canola fields come to life.

Houw Hoek acquired its name due to the challenge that this very difficult portion of the mountain presented for wagons and their passengers, whether descending or ascending. To prevent the laden wagons from toppling over, everyone had to hang on for dear life while the men were instructed to grip the ends of rawhide ropes slung over the wagons in order to hold them back and slow them down. The driver would shout '*Hou op die hoek*' (meaning 'hold on the corner') as the wagon inched its way up or down a few metres on the steep slope. The danger was real enough; some travellers were unlucky, and there were times when an entire team with its wagons plunged over a precipice to their deaths on the perilous ascent. The return journey was even more hazardous. Without brakes, there was the risk of loaded wagons colliding with the rear of the span of oxen, panicking them into plummeting off the track, and thus causing the destruction of both team and wagon. To prevent this, brake-sleds were secured to the wheels to lock them in position so that the wagon could ease down the slope like a sled.

Nowadays, the road cutting through this once deadly mountain pass is a modern dual carriageway with a sweeping vista over the valley. Here the route bypasses the village of Bot River, one of the first designated loan farms in the Overberg, before continuing into the low-lying agricultural lands. The fields are dry in summer, but in winter the green pastures are quilted with bright yellow canola fields and often overarched by dazzling rainbows. Bot River, once the trading post between early settlers at the Cape and the indigenous Khoikhoi tribes, and named for the butter that was a staple of the trade, lies approximately 30 kilometres from Hermanus.

An alternative way to get to Hermanus is along the Cape Whale Coast Route. This meandering route follows the R44 and traverses the Kogelberg Biosphere Reserve. The road takes you along the coastline of False Bay, so named because early sailors approaching from the east were sometimes deceived by Cape Hangklip's resemblance to Cape Point. Although it may take slightly longer to arrive at your destination, the Cape Whale Coast Route is a visual experience not to be missed.

As you follow the coast, you will come to the naval village of Gordon's Bay, lying higgledy-piggledy between the Atlantic Ocean and the Hottentots Holland Mountains. In the early days of the Cape settlement, Gordon's Bay was renowned for good fishing (the original name of the area was Vishoek), and its first tenant had to furnish the Governor with an annual allotment of 200 oysters as part of the rental. The village was later named after Colonel Robert Gordon, the last commander of the garrison of the Dutch East India Company.

Above the harbour and Bikini Beach promenade, the slopes are adorned with historic fishermen's cottages as well as modern, opulent homes climbing the contours to claim superb marine vistas. The towering peaks here are so close to the sea that the narrow road winds through the village before taking you onto spectacular Clarence Drive, as it runs between the mountain face and the sheer drops to the ocean.

Clarence Drive, stretching over 21 kilometres, with its 77 bends and curves and its vast dramatic wilderness of seascapes and mountains, has been voted one of the best panoramic drives in the world. It was named after G. J. V. (Jack) Clarence, a director of the Cape Hangklip Beach Estate Company, 'whose vision, faith and determination helped to bring the road into being'. The road was constructed by Italian prisoners of war in World War II.

Lay-by sightseeing points along this route afford unsurpassed vistas from False Bay to Cape Point. A highlight between June and December is to catch a glimpse of whales breaching or a school of dolphins leaping in formation through the waves.

The Cape Whale Coast Route stretches out in a winding ribbon that threads through the far-flung villages dotted along the Atlantic seaboard. Skirting the spectacular mountain range, the trajectory of your journey takes you through a vast expanse of remote territory before sweeping towards the treacherous ocean at Koeëlbaai (Kogel Bay, meaning 'cannonball bay'). The bay's Dutch name refers to the loud crashing of boulders that can be heard in strong storms. Here the sea is known for its dangerous rip currents and shipwrecks, not to mention a healthy population of great white sharks. Even so, the bay, with its kilometres of unfurling waves, is popular with surfers.

Colonel Robert Gordon

From here, the road retreats inland as it rises at the river mouth near a secluded hamlet, Rooi-Els ('red alder'), to follow a mountain pass where the escarpment transforms into a natural biosphere of wild flowers and proteas. Some 1,800 indigenous plant species flourish on the brooding mountain slopes, buffeted by robust sea gales.

The Kogelberg Biosphere Reserve, which encompasses the Kogelberg Nature Reserve, covers an expanse of 100,000 hectares, of which 70,000 hectares are terrestrial and the rest marine. The reserve, proclaimed by UNESCO (United Nations Educational, Scientific and Cultural Organisation) in 1998, was the first internationally recognised biosphere reserve in South Africa. Today, it is part of a global network of more than 600 internationally recognised biosphere reserves. Seventy-seven plant species found here occur nowhere else in the world.

With its great floral wealth and natural beauty, this biosphere reserve is also part of a World Heritage Site, and forms the majestic backdrop to a sustainable 'green' development – Oudebosch, a mountain camp with environment-friendly rustic cabins and an eco-pool. Way off the beaten track, it is an idyllic getaway for nature lovers.

Above: The five eco-cabins at Oudebosch, in the heart of the Kogelberg Nature Reserve between Betty's Bay and Kleinmond, were constructed from wood, glass and stone gabions and are linked by wooden walkways.

Left: The 100,000-hectare Kogelberg Biosphere Reserve is home to more than 1,800 indigenous plant species.

22 HERMANUS

Further along, the road continues to climb towards Pringle Bay, a small coastal town named for Sir Thomas Pringle of the British Navy, who commanded the Cape Station in 1796. Pringle Bay nestles at the foot of the Hangklip Mountain, whose name refers to the 'hanging rock' that appears to cling to its slopes. During the eighteenth century, the mountain caves were inhabited by indigenous tribes, and were also the hideout of slaves escaping from their colonial masters. A short stroll takes you to the Cape Hangklip Lighthouse where it keeps vigil on the eastern tip of False Bay. This solitary region, incessantly pounded by strong winds, is legendary for its nautical graveyard of shipwrecks, and for those unfortunate fishermen swept from the rocks by treacherous and unpredictable waves.

The route continues to wind inland, following the lower slopes of the mountains, dominated by high sandstone peaks. The rugged landscape, barnacled with boulders, is home to the sprawling coastal village of Betty's Bay, named after Betty Youlden, daughter of the managing director of the first company to attempt development of the Cape Hangklip area. The whole area surrounding the village was once a retreat for runaway slaves who sought sanctuary in the mountains from the oppression of their owners. Dr Hendrik Verwoerd, the former prime minister of South Africa and architect of apartheid, who was assassinated in 1966, once owned a holiday home here; a small memorial stands in his memory.

A gateway to the Kogelberg Biosphere Reserve is the Harold Porter National Botanical Garden, set between mountain and sea in Betty's Bay. The garden is an exceptional sanctuary of indigenous plant life. The early Dutch settlers called the indigenous vegetation growing at the southern tip of Africa *fijnbosch* (fynbos), meaning 'fine-leafed bush'. Fynbos consists of proteas, ericas, restios, grasses, and a variety of other plant types and geophytes (which include gladioli, lilies and orchids). These unique and hardy plants of the Cape, collectively known as the Cape Floristic Region, have

The Kleinmond Lagoon at daybreak. In summer it is a hive of activity, with locals and holidaymakers gathering here to play, swim, canoe, boardsail or sunbathe.

evolved over the centuries to survive in the nutrient-poor soil, high winds, dry summers and wet winters that characterise the region. More than 8,600 species have been recorded in this fynbos ecoregion, which is known to contain the greatest concentration of wild flowers in the country.

The tranquil Harold Porter botanical garden, with its cascading waterfalls and deep pool gorges, is a delight for lovers of fauna and flora. Depending on the time of year, you can spot South Africa's national flower, the king protea. The garden also offers spectacular walks and low-impact activities, which include birding, wild-flower harvesting, mountain biking and hiking along scenic trails. Its *Creature Catalogue* lists an amazing diversity of fauna, ranging from tiny insects like bugs, beetles and spiders to large mammals such as leopards and chacma baboons.

Betty's Bay is also home to a colony of African penguins at the Stony Point Nature Reserve. The African penguin is listed as one of the three most critically endangered bird species in the Western Cape. Apart from natural predators, major threats to the welfare of seabirds are pollution, oil spills and long-line fishing. The protection and conservation of rare and endangered bird species is the primary mission of the organisation BirdLife South Africa.

The ruins of the old Southern Cross Whaling Station, founded in 1912, can also be seen at Stony Point.

Following the tongue of the road along the coast, you will soon reach the town of Kleinmond ('little mouth'), lying between two lagoons: the Palmiet River Mouth and the Bot River Vlei. In the days of the ox wagon and the paraffin Tilley lamp, this seaside spot was a popular resort for *dominees* (church ministers) and farmers from the districts of Caledon and Elgin in the Overberg, who made it their annual fishing holiday destination. Today, development has created an established and busy centre with its own small harbour and infrastructure of commerce and industry.

The Leopard's Kloof Trail is one of three trails in the Harold Porter National Botanical Garden in Betty's Bay.

One of the largest African penguin breeding colonies in the world can be found at Stony Point Nature Reserve.

Together the four resorts of Rooi-Els, Pringle Bay, Betty's Bay and, the largest of the four, Kleinmond all form part of the Kogelberg Biosphere Reserve.

The Cape Whale Coast Route, with its picturesque jigsaw arrangement of seaside villages, beckons to those choosing to live 'off the grid'. Far from city lights, country adventurers map out their territory – a niche in which they are free to follow their creative passions as artists, writers or artisans in home industries. One example is Gaspard Bossut, a Belgian *chocolatier de luxe* who knows that chocolate feeds the soul; he handcrafts each truffle to perfection at GaBoli Chocolates in Betty's Bay. A visit to his home factory will be a highlight on your journey.

As the road leaves Kleinmond, it takes you on a rustic inland detour towards the exclusive Arabella Country Estate. Here, the stylish natural architectural theme includes a five-star hotel and premier spa flanked by upmarket private homes. Surrounded by the Kogelberg Mountains, Arabella is home to one of the most prestigious golf courses in South Africa, where the fairways, fringed with fynbos, blend in seamlessly with the environment.

The Arabella Hotel and Spa overlooks the Bot River Lagoon near the Rooisand Reserve, which forms the eastern coastal border of the Kogelberg Biosphere Reserve. The wetlands here are a paradise for many species of aquatic and land-based birds, including flamingos and pelicans, as well as a herd of wild horses. Legend has it that these horses are descended from British mounts released at the end of the Anglo-Boer War in 1902. Another version holds that their ancestors were horses released into the marshes by Dutch farmers to avoid requisition by the British during that same war.

Once past the Arabella Country Estate, the road meets the R43 as you start the final lap of your journey to Hermanus. In the approach to the coast, the farmlands give way to rolling slopes covered in a rising vista of vineyards bordering the Bot River Lagoon. Reminiscent of a Mediterranean landscape, the Benguela Cove Wine Estate thrives in an impressive setting of vines, olive groves and lavender fields. The sweeping views of the ocean and mountains from this estate, with its state-of-the-art winery, are magnificent. Seventy hectares of the land here are dedicated to a private wildlife reserve where grey rhebok, duiker, grysbok and other indigenous game can be seen.

Approximately 15 kilometres further is Hermanus, the largest town in the Overberg, and the whale capital of the world.

Surrounded by the Kogelberg Mountains, the picturesque Arabella Golf Course ranks among the top ten courses in South Africa.

AN OVERVIEW

'To understand Hermanus as it is today, with its undoubted but elusive charm, it is necessary to turn back the pages of the past; to see how Hermanus came to be what it is today – and who influenced its progress.'

Jose Burman, *Hermanus – A Guide to the Riviera of the South*, 1989

What is it about Hermanus that draws people from far and wide to settle here, or to spend their golden days in this charming town?

Can it really be that a formerly impoverished little fishing hamlet with the ridiculous name of Hermanuspietersfontein has sparked an accumulation (at a conservative estimate) of R4,000 million in property values, and is still a small town?

Since its early days as an angler's paradise, Hermanus has grown into a flourishing town and holiday resort.

HERMANUS 29

The history

'The bontebocks, above all, appeared in flocks of two thousand at least. I am persuaded that this day, buffaloes, antelopes of all kinds, zebras and ostriches, I had before my eyes at one time more than four or five thousand animals.'

François Levaillant, explorer and naturalist,
travelling in the Overberg in 1796

Long before progress and urbanisation claimed the land, wild game abounded in ancient milkwood forests and lush vegetation spreading down to the coastline at the tip of Africa.

The archives record the story of Hermanus Pieters, a teacher from Holland who taught Dutch to the children at Boontjieskraal, a farm close to Caledon and once the site of the kraal of Jan Buntjie, a Khoisan leader. In the 1800s, when the English language became compulsory in government schools at the Cape, the Dutch (Afrikaans) farmers started their own schooling system, and brought out teachers from Holland. Hermanus Pieters was paid with sheep, and during the holiday period he embarked on a journey with his flock in search of fresh grazing. Pieters followed the Elephant Path, travelling through the Hemel-en-Aarde (meaning 'heaven and earth') Valley before climbing over the Raed-na-Gael Mountain to the coast. It seems that he may have heard about this route from one of the farming families he visited in the district, or perhaps at the leper colony that was established in the valley in 1817.

The Riviera Hotel was built in 1904. In 1908 it was bought by local businessman and 'hotelier par excellence' Pieter John Luyt, who also owned the Marine Hotel.

HERMANUS 31

Hermanus histories

Late in the eighteenth century, Hendrik Cloete of the farm Nooitgedacht, near Stellenbosch, built the first holiday home in Hermanus. The homestead, known as the 'Mondhuis', was built at the Klein River Mouth, on the eastern boundary of the Mosselrivier farm, which had been used for grazing since 1724. On her travels, Lady Anne Barnard and her entourage stopped at the Cloete house to rest their horses and have lunch.

S. J. du Toit, Hermanus Stories I, 2001

Early Hermanus, seen from Hoy's Koppie to the east.

Once he had crossed the summit, the trailblazing teacher/shepherd looked down on a windswept and primitive landscape, where waterfalls and streams ran their course to the sea. He set up camp for his sheep beside a freshwater spring, close to the cliff's edge and the waves breaking over the rocks.

The excellent grazing and water supply inspired the teacher to repeat his 'shepherd safari' each summer. In a tranquil spot, far from the classroom, he could enjoy fishing while also exploring the uncharted territory of the coastline.

Hermanus Pieters died at Boontjieskraal farm in 1837, but it was his destiny to lend his name to the site of the spring. According to folklore, the spring was named Hermanus Pieters se Fonteyn ('fountain of Hermanus Pieters) by the settlers' children, whose duty it was to collect buckets of water from this source.

The news of the spring and abundant summer vegetation encouraged farming families residing in the interior to make the seaside spot an annual destination. Travelling by ox wagon with their livestock on an arduous and lengthy journey, they would set up camp on the cliffs just as the pioneering Boontjieskraal shepherd had once done.

And so it was that settlement and development began. In 1854, 12 plots on Crown land, situated near the spring, were sold at a public auction in Caledon for one pound and four shillings each; the sale was registered the following year. A fisherman, Johannes Michiel Henn, wishing to find a safe harbour, travelled with his wife, Henrietta, their five sons, five daughters and their spouses, from Harry's Bay seven miles down the coastline, to settle at Hermanuspietersfontein in 1857. It was Henn who built the first cottage in 1860.

Fishermen plied their trade from this rocky cove. It became the site of the first harbour in Hermanus, today known as the Old Harbour.

The Old Harbour, *circa* 1904. The Marine Hotel can be seen in the background.

Soon, reports of the small seaside village with its long name and prolific marine life reached Cape Town.

An early postmaster, Mr Gift, complained about the effort of writing the long name 'Hermanuspietersfontein'. During 1902, as a labour-saving measure, he took the decision to lop off the last bit – an innovative move and a 'gift' in itself for the village, which thenceforth was known simply as Hermanus, the official name we have today.

A popular highlight was the kabeljou (kob) run from November through to March, when the cliffs were transformed into a forest of fishing rods, with anglers vying for a good place on the rocks to cast their lines. The coastal waters of Hermanus became a harvest ground for red steenbras, stumpnose, kabeljou, galjoen and musselcrackers. Well-known fishing spots included Kwaaiwater ('angry waters'), Sievers Point and Die Gang ('the alley'). From 1910 to the 1940s, Hermanus had a reputation as an anglers' paradise. In those days, fishermen had their pick of the fish, and because the bounty of the ocean seemed endless, no thought was given to conservation. Long before the mass exploitation of the fisheries and deep-water trawling, with its indiscriminate and devastating effect on the marine ecology, there was a time when a fisherman in Hermanus could catch as many as 30 to 40 fish a day.

Times have changed. Today, strict environmental control has been implemented in an attempt to sustain the delicate balance of marine life along the South African coast.

'King of the game-fish hunters'

A fisherman known as the 'king of the game-fish hunters' once spent five hours landing a monster shark. The epic adventure of Bill Selkirk, the owner of a local bait shop, took place on a mellow day in April 1922. He scrambled across rocks, through gullies, and up and down the clifftops to land the whopping great blue pointer, using only his 12-foot Cape bamboo rod. At times the 800-metre line was fully extended out to sea, and the tin float was so close to the shark that one slash of its lethal teeth would have crushed it; if that had happened, the shark would undoubtedly have escaped.

Practically the entire village downed tools on that memorable afternoon, with the locals lining the clifftops to cheer on their hero as he wrestled with his opponent. Finally, at sunset, Bill sensed the giant shark tiring. Himself numb with fatigue, he resolutely held on until he managed to draw his flagging adversary into the shallow mouth of the Old Harbour. A noose was cast around its tail and the battle was over.

The blue pointer was almost twice as big as anything previously caught on a rod and line. But because the fisherman had used a float, the catch was disqualified as a world record. Bill Selkirk's reasonable objection to this was that rival catches had been made from boats, which could be manoeuvred and were in fact far more helpful to a fisherman than a float was to a rock angler.

Selkirk's feat was published in newspapers across the globe and a photograph of his record shark was featured in colour in the *Illustrated London News*. His exploits so impressed General Jan Smuts, then prime minister of South Africa, that he visited the legendary angler on several trips to Hermanus. However, Zane

The legendary Bill Selkirk, known as the 'king of the game-fish hunters'.

Grey, writer of Wild West novels as well as a master big-game angler, dismissed the story, saying that it was impossible for a shark to be hooked and landed on that tackle – or for that matter on any tackle; and he promptly cancelled his proposed trip to Hermanus.

Thus the name of Bill Selkirk, a modest fisherman, went down in history as a champion angler – maybe the greatest ever. Bill's other claim to fame was his family connection with Alexander Selkirk, better known as Robinson Crusoe!

The Victoria Hotel was built in the late 1880s, providing accommodation for an increasing number of holidaymakers and fishermen attracted by the abundance of marine life in Walker Bay.

A quiet town

As the seaside resort of Hermanus grew in popularity, J. O. Rowe, editor of the recently established *Hermanus News*, expressed his views in December 1949 about the future of this peaceful place:

I hope with all my heart that Hermanus will not become a city of casinos and gin palaces, of great pavilions blocking out the glory of the seacoast; of wide concrete parades reflecting the heat of the sun and burning the eyes; of great motor roads tempting the young road-hog to devil-may-care antics with blasting of horns and screeching of brakes. There are other parts of the coast more suitable for attracting the noisy 'must-let-off-steam' bunch.

Anyway, Hermanus does not seem to be geographically suited for such attraction, for mercifully it is not on the way to anywhere special.

Hermanus seems to me to be in an almost unique position in South Africa for forming a sanctuary, not only for fauna and flora, but also for the development of the natural creative and artistic habits, which find little opportunity for expression in this country.

In this quiet town, there are signs already of people with vision making their homes or business premises into places of rest and beauty; there are artists who are working for its sake ...

The heyday of hotels

'Hermanus combined, in those days, all the pleasure of an open-air life and an unspoilt coastline with the picturesqueness of a small fishing village and the comfort of modern well-run hotels with personal service and good food.'

Berdine Luyt (edited by Robin Lee), *In Those Days – The Story of Joey Luyt and the Marine Hotel*, 2014

As Hermanuspietersfontein developed into a village, visitors wanting accommodation could rent rooms in a stone cottage on the seafront, known as the Strandhuis ('beach house'). At the same time, the settlement's infrastructure began to expand; more shops were established and commercial activity increased. A pioneering Scotsman, Walter McFarlane, who had started a fishing business in thé town, opened the first hotel, known as the Victoria Hotel. He was also to become the first mayor of Hermanus. The increasing number of holidaymakers from Cape Town and the surrounding towns would soon create a need for further hotel accommodation.

Hermanus became fashionable in a heyday of hotels, attracting tourists who would leave the harsh northern winters to enjoy summer months of leisure alongside the shores of Walker Bay. Because of the town's healing air, a sanatorium was built on Marine Drive in 1896. This establishment was owned by Dr Josua Hoffman, brother-in-law to Jan Christiaan Smuts, who would later become prime minister of South Africa. It became a frequent place of retreat for Smuts, who usually took an early-morning dip at Fick's Pool nearby.

Hermanus histories

In 1915 Hermanus, on the south-western coast of South Africa, was an insignificant fishing village. By 1947 it was one of the pre-eminent sea-side holiday resorts in the country, and well-known abroad. There were several reasons for this: a healthy climate; unequalled sea-angling; beautiful natural countryside and steadily improving road access. The town was also blessed with entrepreneurial citizens, who saw the value of 'eco-tourism' long before this became a catch phrase. At one stage in the 1930s Hermanus boasted 13 hotels.

Berdine Luyt, edited by Robin Lee, *In Those Days – The Story of Joey Luyt and the Marine Hotel*, 2014

The Ocean View Hotel was one of several reputable establishments that offered holidaymakers full board and lodging during their stay in Hermanus.

The Bay View Hotel's 'Gin Alley'.

With the growing demand for accommodation, the sanatorium was later bought by an entrepreneur, David Allen. He converted it to the Windsor Hotel, which he named after the mailship in memory of his seafaring experiences to and from the United Kingdom. The gabled building looking out over the cliffs is one of the best-known historical landmarks of the town.

However, one of the most prestigious hotels in present-day Hermanus is undoubtedly The Marine. It was built, and owned, by business partners Walter McFarlane and Valentine Beyers after the Anglo-Boer War ended in 1902. Even back then, this hotel was far more sophisticated than the Victoria Hotel, also owned by McFarlane. When the partnership between the two men ended in 1915, McFarlane retained the Victoria and Beyers kept the Marine, which was placed under the management of his son-in-law, Pieter John Luyt. During the 1940s, when still in the ownership of the Luyt family, the hotel was renamed Luyt's Marine Hotel.

In the 1920s, the Marine Hotel, with its marvellous ballroom, became the glamorous destination of many affluent and titled visitors from both the United Kingdom and Europe, who referred to the town as the 'Riviera of the South'. Besides royalty, other famous visitors to Hermanus were people like John Galsworthy, author of *The Forsyte Saga*, and E. H. Sheppard, the illustrator of A. A. Milne's well-loved and popular Winnie-the-Pooh books. This was a time when the protocol for hotel guests commanded full evening dress. Women, stylish in the fashion of the day, adorned with jewels and furs, were escorted alongside men attired in dinner jackets and stiffly starched shirts. The attractions of a coastal resort such as Hermanus created many an occasion to celebrate, and during the Christmas season parties were held every night. Festivities ranged from romantic moonlight picnics and campfires in the veld to bridge and card parties, as well as organised and impromptu concerts that provided much fun and entertainment.

In 2017, The Marine – along with two other hotels, The Cellars-Hohenort in Cape Town and The Plettenberg in Plettenberg Bay – was purchased by James B. Sherwood, founder and chairman emeritus of Belmond Ltd, owners of the Mount Nelson Hotel in Cape Town. The three hotels, formerly owned by the McGrath family, are now managed by a newly formed company, the Liz McGrath Collection (Pty.) Ltd, named in memory of the woman who had developed the hotels and devoted her later years to their highly successful operation. All three establishments have been members of the prestigious Relais & Chateaux group.

Another prominent hotel, the Birkenhead, incorporating an old residential home, stood on the cliffs close to Voëlklip Beach. It opened its doors in 1952, and a regular feature was the mid-week arrival of a luxury railway bus at the hotel, bringing overseas tourists to enjoy the famous Birkenhead lunches. On Saturday evenings there was dancing on the terrace overlooking the ocean. For Christmas and New Year meals, the dining room was reputedly booked for at least three sittings. The fame of this luxury hotel as the 'in place' to visit spread all over South Africa and abroad.

A fire in 1969 destroyed one wing of the building. Not long after extensive renovations were made to the hotel it was sold to a syndicate which planned on erecting 32 sectional title units on the site. The hotel was demolished in 1989, but before the construction of the apartments started there was a slump in the market and the land remained vacant until two houses were eventually built where the beautiful hotel had once stood. In 2003, the property owners, Phil and Liz Biden, opened Birkenhead House, an elegant boutique hotel. With its rare antiques and original art, it has, like its predecessor, become a landmark of Hermanus.

While it was fashionable to stay in the hotels, there would come a time when, because of its ideal location, visitors to Hermanus began building their own holiday homes. Local materials were used and most of the houses had thatched roofs. In July 1959 a devastating fire destroyed 23 homes. Then, in February 1962, a furnace of flames raged across the golf course ahead of 70-mile-an-hour north-westerly winds. Twenty-five houses were engulfed, and 22 of them burnt to the ground. In the same year, the town council placed a ban on new construction of thatched roofs. Through the years, hotels also had more than their fair share of fires.

With the approach of a more modern world, Hermanus's grand hotels had to give way to a much wider choice of accommodation options – from boutique hotels, B&B guesthouses and self-catering facilities to camping and backpacker lodges. Nowadays, you will find that there is no shortage of accommodation in Hermanus, and visitors are assured of a wide and competitive selection when choosing the perfect place to suit their requirements. The Hermanus Tourism Bureau, situated at the Old Station Building in town, has detailed information on the type of accommodation available in Hermanus and offers a free booking service.

Hermanus histories

- During the Hermanus 'hotel heyday' the Bay View, with its 83 rooms, was the largest tourist hotel, offering facilities for conferences, wedding receptions and dances for up to 200 persons.
- Back in the 1980s, hotel accommodation prices in Hermanus ranged from R19 bed and breakfast per person (out of season) to R34 bed and breakfast in season. The prestigious Marine Hotel, in 1984, charged rooms from only R38 double (R50 for a suite) out of season ... price-wise those certainly were the good old days!

Nilsson's Central Hotel stood on Main Road, next to the Royal.

HERMANUS HOTELS

According to author Berdine Luyt, at one stage in the 1930s, Hermanus boasted 13 hotels. These hotels of yesteryear were:

- **Bayview Hotel** – Built in 1921. After a fire in 1940, it was rebuilt. In 1985 the hotel was demolished and replaced by Bay View Flats.
- **Birkenhead Hotel** – Built in 1952, but was demolished some years later.
- **Royal Hotel** – Built in 1900; gutted by a fire in 1981.
- **Central Hotel** – Situated next to the Royal Hotel, it also operated under the names of Masonic Hotel, Regent Palace and Nillson's Central Hotel. The building was gutted by fire in 1953.
- **Victoria Hotel** – The first hotel in Hermanus, built in the late 1880s. It was later to become the Astoria but was also destroyed by fire and later rebuilt as a shopping centre.

The *grandes dames* of yesteryear: the Royal (above left), the Riviera (above right), the Cliff Lodge (left), the Windsor (opposite top) and the Marine (opposite bottom).

42   HERMANUS

- **Esplanade Hotel** − Originally known as Stemmet's Private Hotel, built in 1933, but has since been converted into holiday apartments.
- **Seahurst Hotel** − Initially called the Goeie Hoop Losieshuis (Good Hope Boarding House), it was gutted by fire in 1956.
- **Ocean View Hotel** − Demolished in 1970. Today this is the site of Sea Village apartments.
- **Cliff Lodge Hotel** − Gutted by fire during World War II.
- **Riviera Hotel** − Built in 1904. In 1944 the hotel was gutted by a fire. It became the first timeshare establishment in South Africa, but was later demolished for redevelopment.
- **Marine Hotel** − Built in 1902. This grand old lady of Hermanus celebrated its centenary in 2002 and is today a stately five-star hotel and part of the Liz McGrath Collection.
- **Windsor Hotel** − Built in 1896 as a sanatorium. In 1931 it was converted into a hotel. The Windsor has been in the Clark-Brown family since the 1980s.
- **Voëlklip House** − A private hotel and boarding house; it was later turned into holiday flats under sectional title.

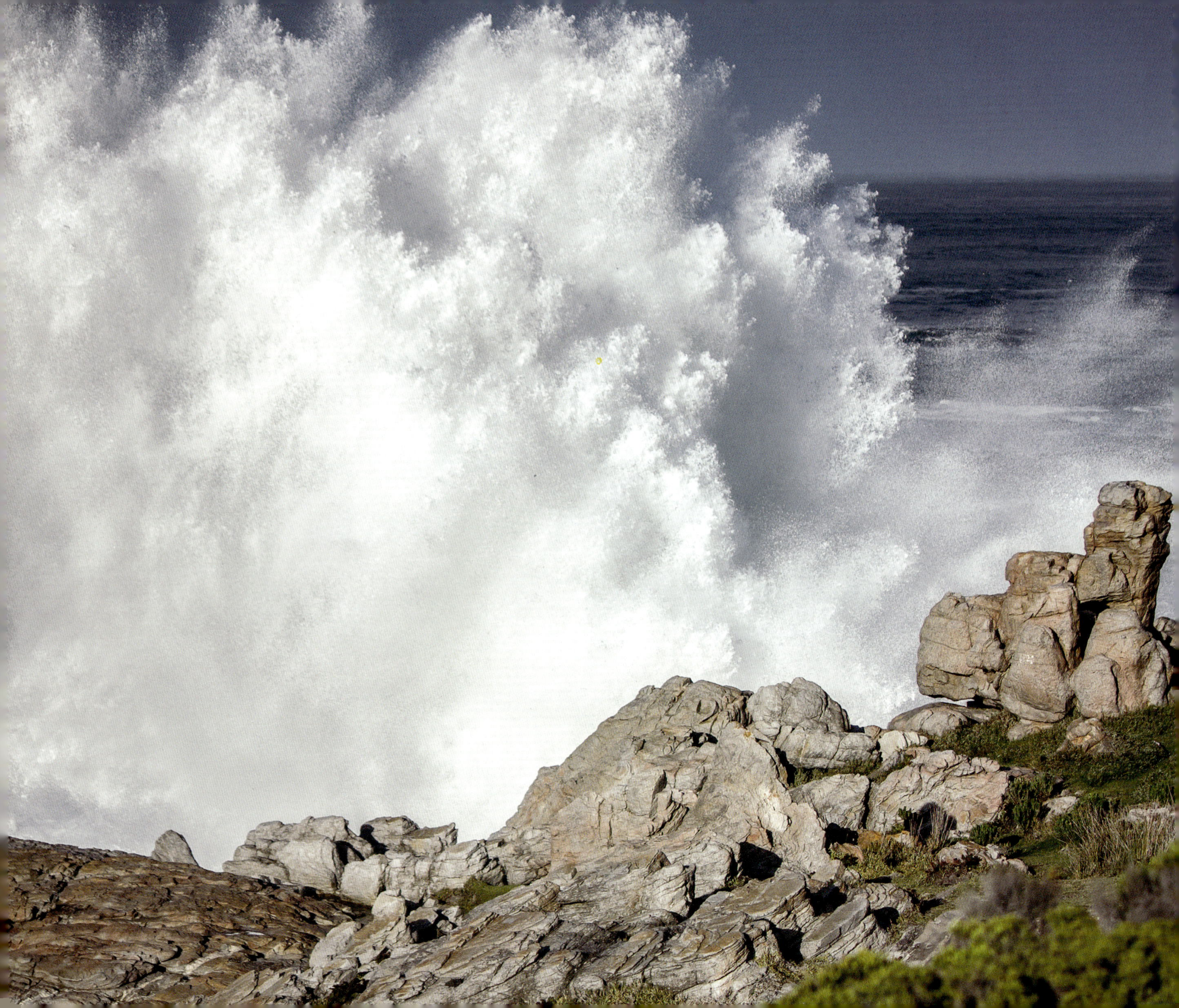

The climate

'The trouble with weather forecasting is that it's right too often for us to ignore it and wrong too often for us to rely on it.'

Patrick Young, writer

Hermanus lies on the Atlantic Ocean near the southernmost tip of Africa, in a triangle of territory bounded by Cape Hangklip in the west, Cape Infanta in the east, and Cape Agulhas in the south. It is at Agulhas that the cold Atlantic meets the warm Indian Ocean.

The climate in Hermanus is similar to that of the Mediterranean. Winter temperatures average 14 degrees Celsius, and in summer the average is 26.4 degrees Celsius. The average annual rainfall is 546 millimetres.

The summers are hot and dry, with robust south-easterly winds in December through to March or April, bringing cooler air from the polar regions. Because the indigenous fynbos vegetation of the region is highly flammable during this season, strong gales can fan fires, which may become uncontrollable in the mountain areas. A 'black south-easter' in Cape Town can carry welcome rain to the Overberg, all the way from Sir Lowry's Pass through to Cape Agulhas, including the Swellendam area. The influence of these winds creates the clear turquoise hue of the ocean with its white-crested waves.

Left: A wave crashes on the mass of rocks at Sievers Point.

Right: Like many fynbos plants, geraniums flower during spring and summer.

The sea temperature is pleasant in summer, until the heavy south-easterly winds arrive, blowing in from the Antarctic and bringing ice-cold water to our shores.

Conversely, in winter, after strong north-westerly gales, the sea temperature rises as the winds bring warmer water down from the equatorial regions. On mellow days, mostly in the autumn months, early morning and afternoon sea mists have made Hermanus renowned for its champagne air.

After winter showers, a technicolour rainbow often arcs the sky, creating a natural luminescent masterpiece across the washed landscape of the Overberg.

Below: Winter's north-westerly gales drive massive waves towards the shore.

Opposite: On some winter mornings, the New Harbour is shrouded in mist, creating an atmospheric ambience.

HERMANUS 47

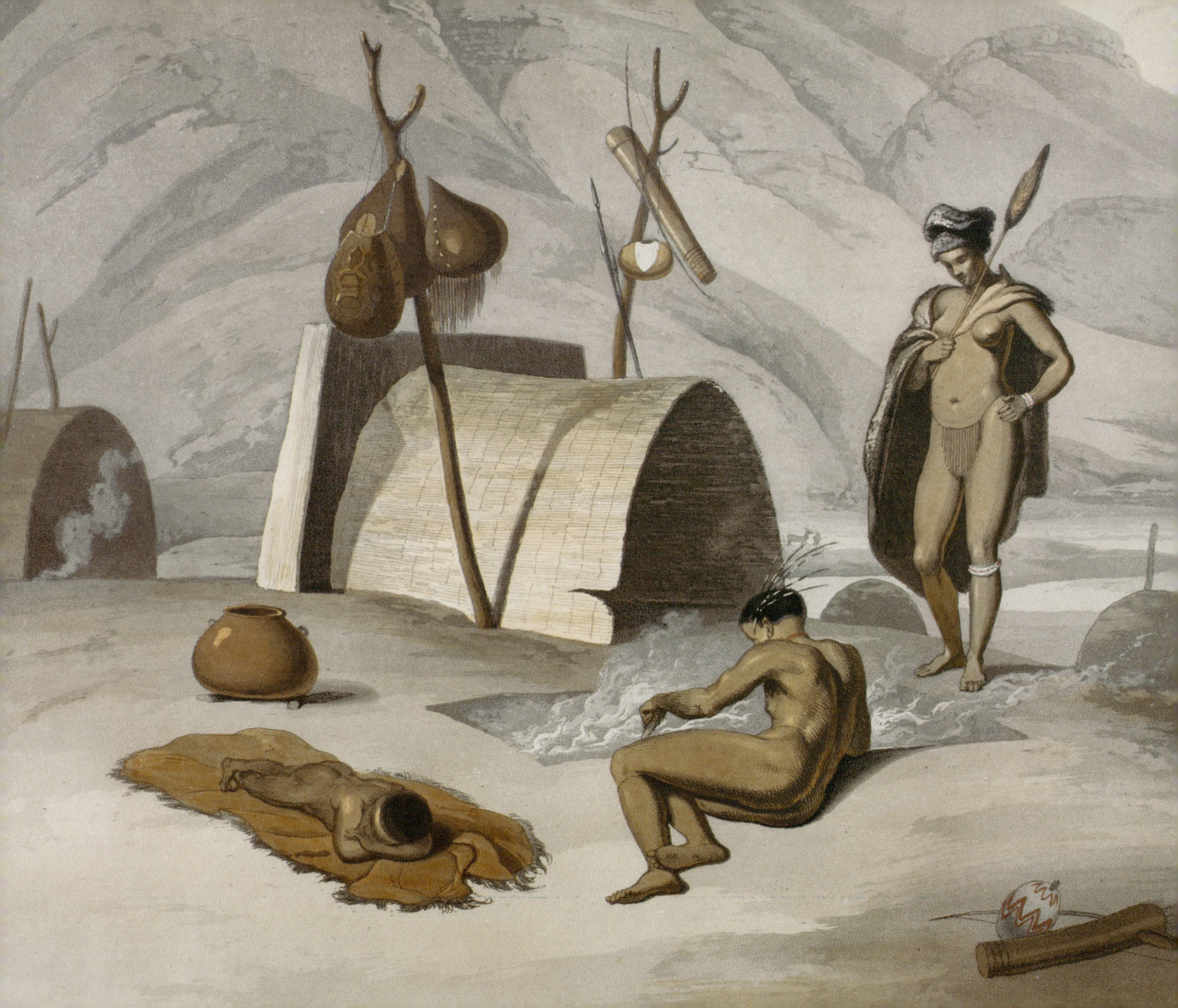

PEOPLE AND PLACES

'The beauty of the world lies in the diversity of its people.'

Nelson Mandela

Prehistory

In the middle of the seventeenth century the people who lived at the Cape included the San people (Bushmen) and the Khoikhoi. 'Khoisan' is the unifying name for the two groups of peoples. The San were hunter-gatherers, whereas the Khoikhoi led a more pastoral life. These people dominated the subcontinent for centuries before the appearance of the first Nguni tribes approximately 1,700 years ago.

The hunter-gatherer San lived in family groups in caves or huts; they wore treated animal skins (karosses) and shell ornaments, and rubbed their skins with fat boiled with the indigenous herb buchu. The men used spears, clubs, and bows and arrows. Groups living next to the sea would eat fish, shellfish, and even dead seals and whales washed up on the beach. Simply by wading into the sea pools, they could catch perlemoen (abalone), oysters and crayfish.

The San adorned the walls of their caves with rock paintings of hunting scenes and spiritual experiences. The name 'San' (also Sanqua or Soaqua) was given to them by the Khoikhoi, and means 'people different from ourselves'. The Dutch called the San *Bossiesmense* (meaning 'bushmen'); both the Khoikhoi and the Dutch regarded them as an inferior people, living off the land without cattle.

Khoikhoi pastoralists arrived in the Western Cape approximately 2,000 years ago. Although this image is of a Khoikhoi group near the Orange River, several groups, or chiefdoms, had moved from the Cape along the southern Cape coast towards modern-day Port Elizabeth.

The Khoikhoi kept herds of cattle and fat-tailed sheep (above).

The Khoikhoi, a more structured society than the San, were nomadic herders. They led a pastoral life, moving from one place to another with their fat-tailed sheep and indigenous cattle. The name 'Khoikhoi' means 'men of men'. However, early Dutch settlers called them 'Hottentots', meaning 'stammerers', because of the clicks and guttural sounds in their language. Today, this term is regarded as offensive.

The tribes, widely scattered and each under its own chief, lived in settlements of portable woven huts, easy to carry when they moved on. They were particularly numerous in the area between the southern mountain ranges and the sea. In the Overberg area, the Khoikhoi lived in kraals at Kleinrivier Kloof and Attaquas Kloof, grazing their sheep and cattle on the coastal lowlands.

The Khoikhoi were the first indigenous people to come into contact with the Dutch settlers at the Cape in the mid-seventeenth century; as so often with such encounters, the result was disastrous for the local population. The tribes bartered their livestock for the white man's alcohol and tobacco, and were steadily dispossessed of their land as the settlers took it over for farms. In 1713, a smallpox epidemic nearly wiped out the entire Khoikhoi population.

Suburbs and settlements

The Hermanus of today is composed of a diversity of cultures. The Coloured people originally made their homes close to the sea, along a strip of coastline once known as Herriesbaai (Harry's Bay). In the early 1800s an African-American from Boston, Samson Dyer, settled close to Gansbaai to harvest fur seals on an island, which was then named after him. When the Cape government decided to take over the offshore islands for guano, they compensated Dyer with four morgen of ground adjoining Herriesbaai. Dyer divided the land and sold the plots for housing. The development was named Hawston in honour of Charles Haw (1819–1871), a civil commissioner of Caledon. The suburb, located between Fisherhaven and Onrus, is one of the oldest settlements in the area and, like Hermanus, has changed dramatically since its humble beginnings. Hawston boasts a beautiful Blue Flag beach as well as an Olympic-sized swimming pool.

Mount Pleasant, set at the foot of Rotary Way, is distinguished by its eclectic mix of vibrantly painted houses. This historic settlement, dating back to 1929, is also one of the older Hermanus suburbs. Many of today's Coloured residents descend from the fishing families of the original village by the sea. With ongoing development, Mount Pleasant today has an infrastructure of shops, schools and a sports field, which is especially popular for weekend matches.

In 1962, under the former government's rule, African people were forcibly evicted from Lower Mount Pleasant and housed in a township named Zwelihle (meaning 'place of beauty'). Zwelihle is the oldest black township in the Overberg.

The first homes were built here in 1963 and included 42 two-roomed dwellings and a hostel for 40 migrant workers. After the airstrip nearby had been closed to air traffic, more housing was created and this development was named Kwasa-Kwasa (meaning 'daybreak').

The small population that lived in huts more than 50 years ago has swelled dramatically today. In 1981 there were 735 residents living in Zwelihle; the current population reputedly stands at 45,000. IsiXhosa is the main language of Zwelihle, but Sesotho and isiZulu are also spoken here.

Above left: Despite the increasing challenges of earning a living from fishing, the people of Hawston are fiercely proud of the place they call home.

Above right: Between Sandbaai and Hermanus lies Mount Pleasant, a neighbourhood of small, colourful houses and warm smiles.

Left: Tour guide Thozamile Stuurman (centre) relaxes with friends at Edongwe Café in Zwelihle.

Opposite: Zwelihle is a hive of activity on most days. Spaza shops offer residents a convenient shopping experience on their doorstep (top), while on some street corners women sell barbecued chicken feet with sauce – a local delicacy (bottom left). In the afternoons, children take to the streets to play (bottom right).

Zwelihle is not a wealthy place, but there is a wealth in the spirit of community. A sense of sharing and social interaction is what you may experience on a township tour. The pulse of the place is evident on the streets in a noisy network of daily commerce: internet cafés, spaza shops, hairdressing salons, and shoe repairs jostle with displays of Chinese imports, vegetables and freshly slaughtered poultry. On practically every corner you will see smoke rising from drums of burning coals where cleaned sheep heads are cooked and sold, as well as braaied chicken feet served with a sauce.

The suburb's two taxi ranks, used by most residents, see a lively buzz of commuters constantly coming and going. Edongwe, a Xhosa name which means 'clay' in English, is a popular coffee shop for the locals. At this social meeting place, patrons can enjoy a sidewalk café ambience in the hub of the township.

It was a pleasure to meet Thozamile Stuurman, local tour guide and owner of Thoza Tours, whose heart is as big as his smile. Thozamile hails from Burgersdorp in the Eastern Cape. He informed me that in the apartheid era, the African people were deprived of their family names because the bureaucrats found

52   HERMANUS

HERMANUS 53

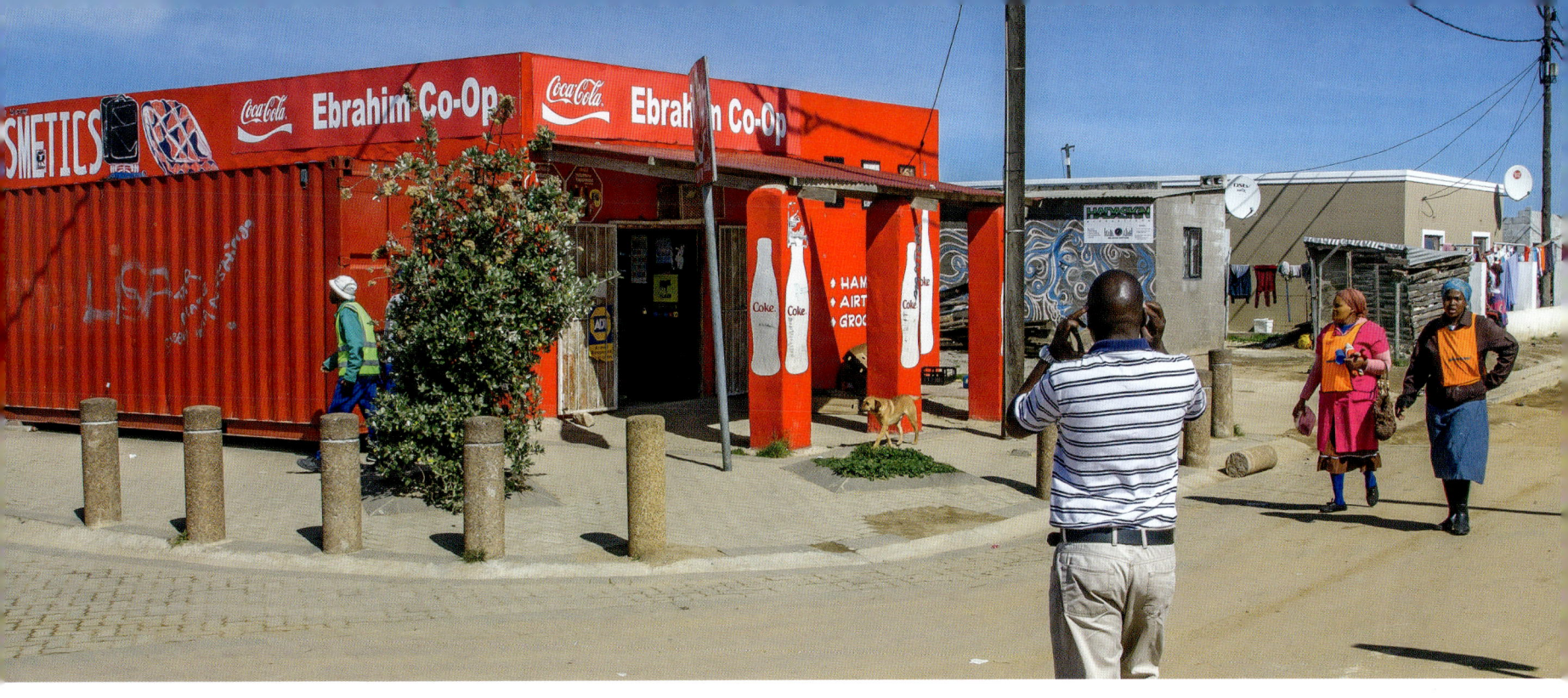

Zwelihle is a mixture of informal dwellings, low-cost housing and middle-class homes.

them too hard to pronounce; instead they were obliged to take on their employer's name. In Thozamile's case, the Afrikaans surname Stuurman was given to his family; he never discovered his authentic family name.

In both Zwelihle and Kwasa-Kwasa, many residents live cheek by jowl in rows of overcrowded little RDP (Reconstruction and Development Programme) houses, wooden shacks, tin shanties and hostel dwellings. Etched on the landscape is a jumble of washing lines with laundry flapping in the wind or washing strewn over fences – amid litter, scruffy dogs and chickens. Electric cables snaking their way across streets bear witness to a bartering system involving the municipal electricity supply. Often unemployed or earning wages well below the breadline, many Zwelihle locals face a daily reality of poverty and disease. Tuberculosis and HIV/Aids are rampant, and basic infrastructure is lacking. Nevertheless, among the residents there is a sense of pride in their heritage and a resilience of spirit that enables them to cope with any adversity that comes their way.

This was confirmed by Thozamile. Innovative entrepreneurs, he told me, wishing for a better life, hire transport containers in which to house their businesses. These containers, once stocked with goods, are called spaza shops. Many rows of such oversized boxes make up a large part of the Zwelihle central business district. The municipality has also erected stalls for commercial retail. Talking to someone like Thozamile, one gets a vivid picture of township life. Living here, he tells me, it is not unusual to see women with 25-litre buckets balanced on their heads, walking from their informal shacks to collect water at the communal ablution block.

Thozamile, wishing to uplift the lives of the impoverished and the less privileged, has become a true ambassador for the community. With the financial assistance of a partner from Holland, he has spearheaded an initiative named 'From Poor to Hope'. This charity provides struggling families with gifts of groceries and money for medication. 'As a community we look after one another,' Thozamile says, adding that the essence of African culture is embodied in the word *ubuntu*, with its message of generosity towards humanity.

Thoza Tours offers the visitor to Zwelihle insight into authentic African lifestyles and folklore, and an opportunity to mingle and exchange cultural views and values with people from local communities.

The Sparklekids initiative, founded by Theodore and Angela Krynauw, inspires and assists Zwelihle youth from disadvantaged homes to reach for their dreams. Through providing mentorship, developing coping skills and creating opportunities towards further studies or jobs through internships, the programme enables the 'sparklekids' to build a better and brighter future and to understand the importance of giving back to the community. The founders' motto is: 'We identify and financially support young people with "sparkle" and an attitude of gratitude to embark on a journey of passion and possibility.'

Although its name translates to 'restless river' in English, Onrus River (Onrusrivier, or simply Onrus) is a delightful suburb situated alongside a tranquil lagoon. From its source, in the high ridges of the Hemel-en-Aarde Valley, the river makes its way down to the sea.

Angela and Theo Krynauw, founders of the Sparklekids initiative, with Amanda Mahlanyana, a participant in the programme, at The Marine hotel.

The beach at Onrus is popular for sunbathing and walks, but swimming can be dangerous because of the backwash and strong currents. Alongside the lagoon, set in a nature conservation area, is the scenic Milkwood Bistro Restaurant.

The coastline follows a craggy crescent in the direction of the Onrus Caravan Park, which was already a favourite camping site in the early 1800s. Nearby, a natural rocky oasis, Davies Pool, provides an idyllic setting for safe bathing.

Close to the Onrus Caravan Park, the Mission House, a historical landmark and reminder of the past, is today the locale of an exclusive art gallery. In earlier times the homestead belonged to the Moravian missionaries from Genadendal. The Cape government in 1823 appointed these missionaries to manage the leper colony in the Hemel-en-Aarde Valley.

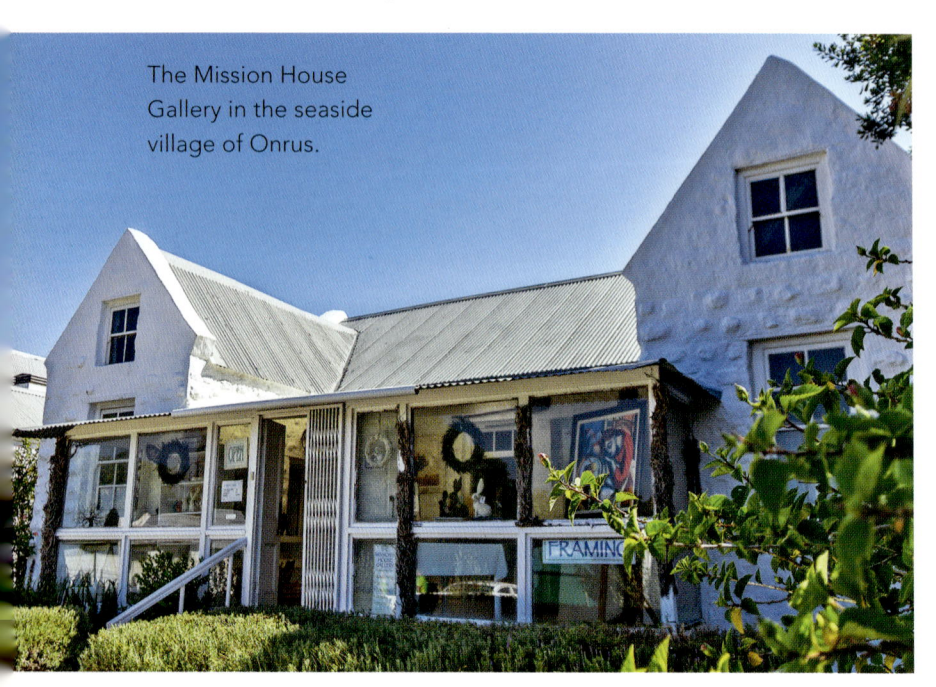

The Mission House is known to have played an important role over the years in the artistic heritage of Onrus. It seems aesthetically fitting that such a legacy continues today in the impressive surrounds of this landmark and in its gallery, where the works of Old Masters and contemporary local artists adorn the walls.

Another feature of Onrus is the tiny St Luke's Greek Orthodox chapel which, in 1998, hosted the wedding ceremony of former South African president F. W. de Klerk and his second wife, Elita, who is of Greek descent.

In 1978 the population in the area consisted of 350 inhabitants. This number has increased considerably over time. Onrus still evokes a sense of country charm at the seaside, and even in such a fast-developing region it seems to retain a spirit of village community. The beauty of its setting has for many years

The Mission House Gallery in the seaside village of Onrus.

Hermanus histories

The Onrus River may have been named for the pounding of the surf on the rocky coast. But there is another version of the name's origins. According to a local historian, the term was used by the Dutch to describe shifting sand at a river mouth between Texel and the North Sea. During Dutch rule of the Cape, they gave the name Onrust to nine places with such shifting sandbanks at a river mouth. The first was at the Eerste River Mouth in 1711, now Macassar. The only one they named Onrust in 1719, and which is still the same, is at the mouth of the Onrus River in the Overberg. It has had the name ever since.

S. J. du Toit, *Hermanus Stories I*, 2002

Part of Vermont's greenbelt system, the salt pan is a gathering place for several species of waterbird, including flamingos.

encouraged well-known South African artists and writers to visit or drop anchor here; hence the vibey creativity of the village, with its interesting mix of sidewalk cafés, shops and galleries.

Adjoining Onrus is the extensive suburb of Vermont, named, like its namesake state in the USA, for its surrounding green mountains. Vermont is also the site of a salt pan, integral to its greenbelt system. This 'critically endangered ecosystem' is a mildly saline wetland with only a floodwater outflow, in a land depression of about 17.5 hectares. The pan has a system of reed-covered feeder wetlands stretching for a kilometre, and its water levels are largely dependent on prevailing groundwater levels. The salt pan is the habitat of wildlife and bird life – up to 600 flamingos frequent its waters, sometimes for close on six months a year. On the eastern edge of the pan there is a milkwood woodland thicket under which marine shell remains can still be found, evidence of the indigenous groups that inhabited this area some 2,000 to 3,000 years ago.

There was a time when Hermanus was referred to as 'old money by the sea'. Entrenched wealth has passed down over the years, especially along Millionaires' Mile, a prestigious enclave of holiday homes and stylish architectural estates bordering on the Cliff Path. Other affluent areas of Hermanus include Kwaaiwater, Fernkloof, Voëlklip and Eastcliff.

Material prosperity is also reflected in more recently developed residential suburbs such as Hermanus Heights and Chanteclair, as well as in prestige golf estates. Other developments include secure lock-up-and-go complexes and gated retirement villages.

Property values can run into millions of rands. The growth of local real estate prices reflects the burgeoning development of Hermanus itself – currently reported as the Western Cape's fastest-growing area after Cape Town.

Foreign investment and immigration add to a potpourri of cultures under the banner of a multiracial South Africa.

58 HERMANUS

THE WHALES OF WALKER BAY

'Watching whales is the ultimate wildlife experience. Who can resist the thrill of a 50-ton southern right whale launching itself into the air and crashing down with a gigantic splash?'

Mike Bruton, *The Essential Guide to Whales in Southern Africa*, 1998

Walker Bay, apparently named for the much-decorated Royal Navy Admiral Sir Baldwin Wake Walker, Bt. (1802–1876), extends from Danger Point in the east to Mudge Point in the west. It is one of several breeding sites frequented by southern right whales along the southern Cape coast, and one of the most popular whale-watching locations in the world.

Although they were occasionally seen in earlier times when they came close inshore, it was only in the 1960s that whales began spending time along the Hermanus coastline, selecting this body of water as a safe place to mate and calve. Walker Bay has since been declared a whale sanctuary, and only licensed whale-watching boats are permitted to use the bay during the whale season. Marine environmentalist Noel Ashton, in his book *A Quick Guide to the Whales of Southern Africa,* writes that South Africa has 'an incredible diversity of whales and dolphins, with over half of the world's species being either present in our waters or passing

Walker Bay is world famous for the hundreds of southern right whales that gather in its shallow waters during the summer months to calve and nurse their young.

through'. The reason for this, he says, is that the South African coastline abuts two great oceanic systems, the warm Indian Ocean and the cold Benguela, part of the Atlantic Ocean. 'Not only do these two oceanic systems support different life forms, but the presence of the polar maritime system south of us means that we encounter many of the great whale species as they migrate between their southern feeding grounds around Antarctica and their more northerly breeding grounds towards the tropics.'

Over 84 whale and dolphin species are found across the oceans of the globe, of which half are either resident in South Africa's waters or visit during the year. These range from the largest animal ever to have lived on earth, the blue whale, which is occasionally seen in our offshore waters, to our winter visitors the southern right and humpback whales, and the many species of dolphins, including the warm-water bottlenose and humpback dolphins and the dusky and Heaviside's dolphins of the Benguela.

'Whalemania' is one of the fastest-growing sectors in the tourism industry. It is estimated that more than 20 million people embark on travels across the globe to marvel at these gentle giants of the deep. In 1992 Hermanus laid claim to the title of whale capital of the world. The town has certainly benefited from this status, placing it on the map for the best land-based whale watching. From the cliffs, whales can be spotted as close as five metres offshore.

Whales are sensitive, large-brained marine mammals, and are not aggressive towards humans. Instead, they usually display curiosity when an encounter takes place. It is a memorable experience to sight these marine leviathans, whether singly or in a pod, or to listen to their sonorous blowing.

It was once believed that whales follow a cycle of feast and famine, feeding during the summer months on dense swarms of plankton, called copepods, found in the cold and stormy waters of Antarctica, before returning to South African shores in winter solely to mate and calve. However, for a number of years, southern right whales have been seen feeding off Cape Columbine – near Paternoster on the west coast of South Africa – in early summer, during the upwelling events when food supply is plentiful in the area.

The whale season begins in winter, usually late in June, and peaks from August through to the end of October. Between November and January, most of the whales have embarked on their migratory journey back to Antarctica.

Whales normally give birth to one calf at a time, even though females may carry up to seven foetuses. The gestation period is about 12 months and the calves are born in the four-month period between June and September. The mother forms a strong bond with her offspring. Research has shown that female whales have a three-year cycle of pregnancy – being pregnant, raising a calf and resting. Whales usually return to the same place to calve but this is not invariable, and some may move their calves from bay to bay even within a single season. Mother and calf stay close inshore during the nursing period, until the calf is big enough to make the journey south. Nursing continues for six months to a year, in which time the calf suckles from a pair of teats situated either side of the mother's genital aperture.

The southern right whale is a baleen whale, one of three species classified as 'right whales' (right for hunting), belonging to the genus *Eubalaena*. Instead of teeth, baleen whales have plates of a hornlike substance, called baleen or whalebone, which they use like a sieve to separate their food from the water. Southern rights are normally black, except for pale brownish 'callosities' on the head and at the tip of the snout, referred to as the bonnet. These are populated by crustacean parasites and fellow travellers called cyamids. Most southern rights have splashes of white on the belly, and some have

An albino whale calf splashes about in the water just off Piet se Klip, close to the Old Harbour. Unlike other southern right whales, it lacks the necessary skin pigment to develop a dark grey or black skin, colours that characterise this species.

62 HERMANUS

Setting off from the New Harbour, boats offering whale-watching trips will take visitors to spots where recent sightings have been recorded. Although southern right whales are the main attraction, humpback whales, Bryde's whales, dolphins, penguins and a variety of seabirds may also be encountered.

white spots or brownish-grey streaks on the back. Occasionally, an albino calf is sighted. By maturity these, too, have darkened, attaining a brindle colour when adult. The southern right also has a broad back without a dorsal fin, and a long arching mouth that begins above the eye. An adult southern right has an average length of about 13.9 metres and an average weight of 40 tons (about ten elephants!). A newborn calf weighs in at about one ton and can be up to six metres in length.

Southern right whales normally swim at 0.5 to 4 kilometres per hour but may reach top speeds of 17 kilometres per hour. Although they have the ability to dive to a maximum depth of over 300 metres, and can hold their breath for 30 minutes, whales cannot live continuously underwater. When they surface to breathe, they expel a funnel of vapour, and it is often this blow which betrays their presence. Their lifespan is thought to exceed 50 years.

WHALE NUMBERS

- There are ten species of baleen whale. The largest is the blue whale – a rorqual (streamlined with pleated skin on the underside), and one of the biggest animals that has ever existed. The migration pattern of the southern right whale (*Eubalaena australis*) shows they travel between Antarctica and the coasts of Africa, South America, Australia and New Zealand.

- Figures from the University of Pretoria Mammal Research Institute's Whale Unit show that the global southern right whale population decreased from an estimated 70,000 to 80,000 animals in the 1770s to about 300 to 400 in 1935, at which point the population received international legal protection.

- Since the 1960s the species has made a steady recovery globally. The world population is currently estimated at about 15,000 individuals, 5,000 of which occur in South African waters.

The Village News, September 2016

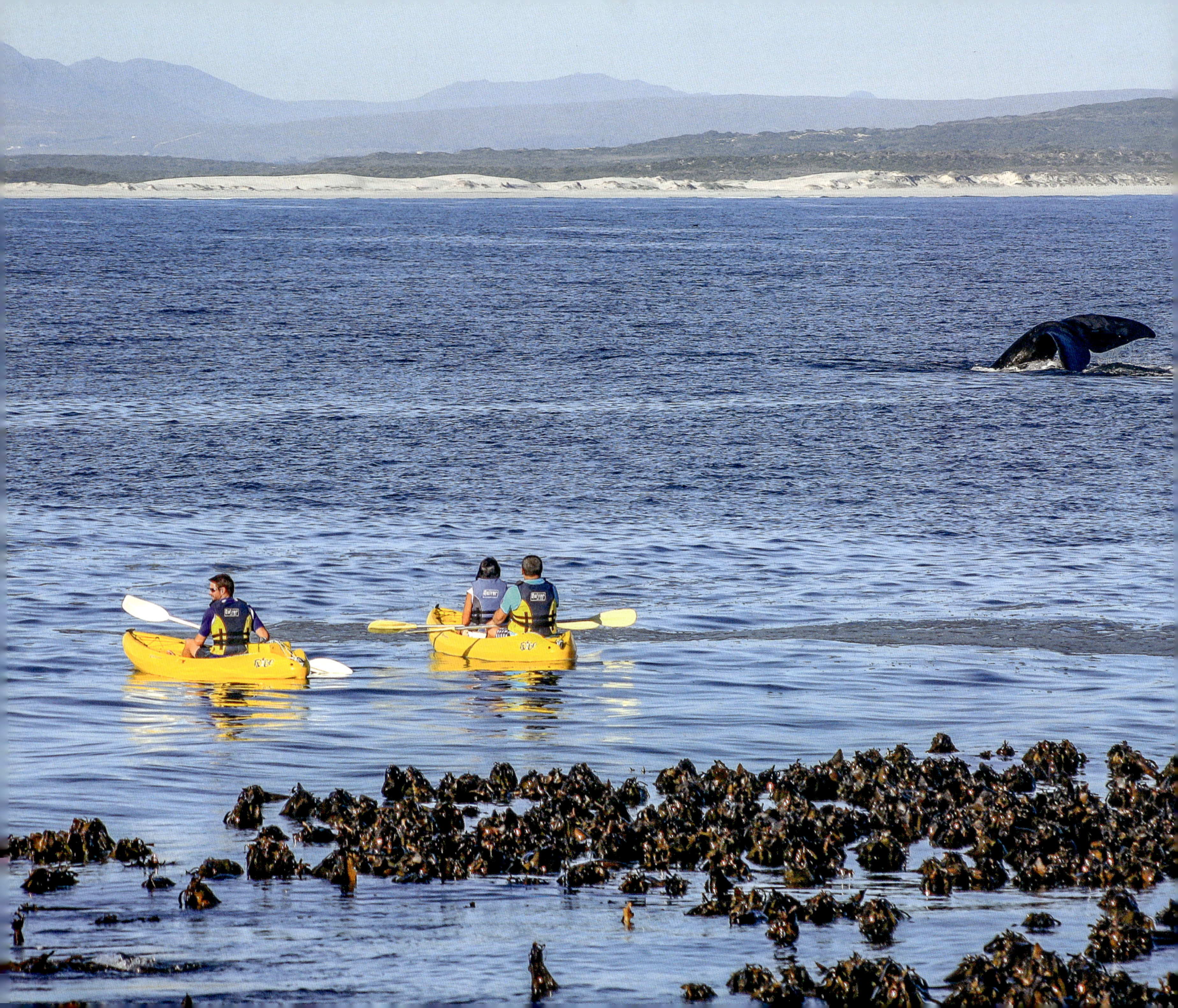

Escaping the freezing waters of Antarctica, southern right whales can be seen in Walker Bay between late June and November. While guided kayaking tours allow paddlers to view the whales from a safe distance (left), those who prefer land-based whale watching can consult the information boards on these winter visitors at Gearing's Point (above).

The history of whaling in southern waters

One of South Africa's foremost marine biologists, Professor Peter B. Best, in his book, *Whale Watching in South Africa: The Southern Right Whale,* documents the dire situation for southern right whales that came about through the commercial whaling industry. Travelling back in time with him, we read:

Historically Right Whales must have been seasonally very abundant in the vicinity of Cape Town, judging by the comments of Van Riebeeck and other early visitors to the Cape, some of whom commented on the commercial potential of the whales (but did little to realise it).

This situation could not last for long. By 1785 whaling vessels from America were overwintering at the Cape, and in 1792 the first Right Whales were taken from the shore by Cape colonists in Table Bay. Between 1785 and 1805 an estimated 12,000 Right Whales were killed along the southern African coast between Walvis Bay and Delagoa (now Maputo) Bay. Nearly all of these were taken by vessels flying American, British or French flags, and at the peak of the fishery there may have been as many as 65 such vessels operating at one time on the coast, each carrying three or four whaleboats which were launched each morning at first light and rowed or sailed around the bays in search of their prey.

Given this concentrated effort, and the fact that the principal targets of the whalers were mothers with calves, it is not surprising that catches (and the population) rapidly collapsed. Nevertheless, because of the high value of a whale (up to 250 pounds sterling in 1830, for instance) and the low cost of catching it, the shore-based fishery continued unabated throughout the 19th and into the early 20th century, with stations operating from time to time in St Helena Bay, Table Bay, False Bay, Mossel Bay, Plettenberg Bay and Algoa Bay. The last recorded attempt to take a Right Whale in South African waters from an open boat with a hand harpoon occurred in False Bay in 1929, by which time an estimated 1,580 Right Whales had been taken from the shore by South Africans – a minor fraction of the total kill by all nations from this stock.

Modern whaling, using steam-powered steel-hulled catchers with a harpoon cannon mounted in the bows, began in South African waters in 1908, and by 1938 a further 84 Right Whales had been killed from land stations at Durban, Saldanha Bay, Hangklip, Mossel Bay and Plettenberg Bay. This low catch (an average of less than three a year), despite relatively advanced catching technology and a continued high demand for the species, indicates that the Right Whales had reached an extremely low level after a century and a half of exploitation.

A whaling station in Table Bay, *circa* 1832. It is estimated that as many as 12,000 southern right whales were killed between 1785 and 1805 in southern Africa.

The plight of the Right Whale, along with some of the other great whales, eventually came to the attention of the international community in the 1920s. In 1931 the signing of a League of Nations 'Convention for the Regulation of Whaling' in Geneva gave complete protection to all Right Whales. This protection came into effect in 1935, and was perpetuated in subsequent international agreements in 1937 and 1946, but only the last included all the major whaling nations.

Although the Right Whales are supposed to have been protected by all the major whaling nations for at least the last 50 years, violations of the protection are known to have taken place, most notably by factory ships belonging to the Soviet Union, which secretly took some 3,200 Southern Right Whales between 1948/1949 and 1970/1971!

South Africa was not entirely innocent, however, and is herself known to have made a few, undeclared catches of Right Whales in the early 1950s.

Fortunately Southern Right Whales seem to have been able to withstand this level of 'poaching', and since the early 1970s have been staging a remarkable comeback.

But the southern right and other whales are by no means out of trouble. More recently, the International Fund for Animal Welfare (IFAW) has requested governments around the world to take a stand against Japan's 'scientific' whaling fleet. The fleet has returned to Southern Ocean waters and to date is responsible for the deaths of 333 whales in a whale sanctuary. There is also a call for a new sanctuary to be created in the South Atlantic Ocean.

Natural predators of whales are sharks and killer whales. Other threats include pollution, net entanglement and ship strikes.

The whale crier

Hermanus has the only whale crier in the world. Between June and November, he takes centre stage in alerting and directing tourists to the sighting of whale pods. This 'Pied Piper' of Walker Bay wears a distinctive hat with a large feather and blows on a long kelp horn. His sandwich board tells whale watchers how to interpret the morse code of the horn to find where the whales have been sighted and how many may be seen. He is usually to be found in the environs of the Old Harbour and around Gearing's Point.

Hermanus's official whale crier, Ricardo Andrews.

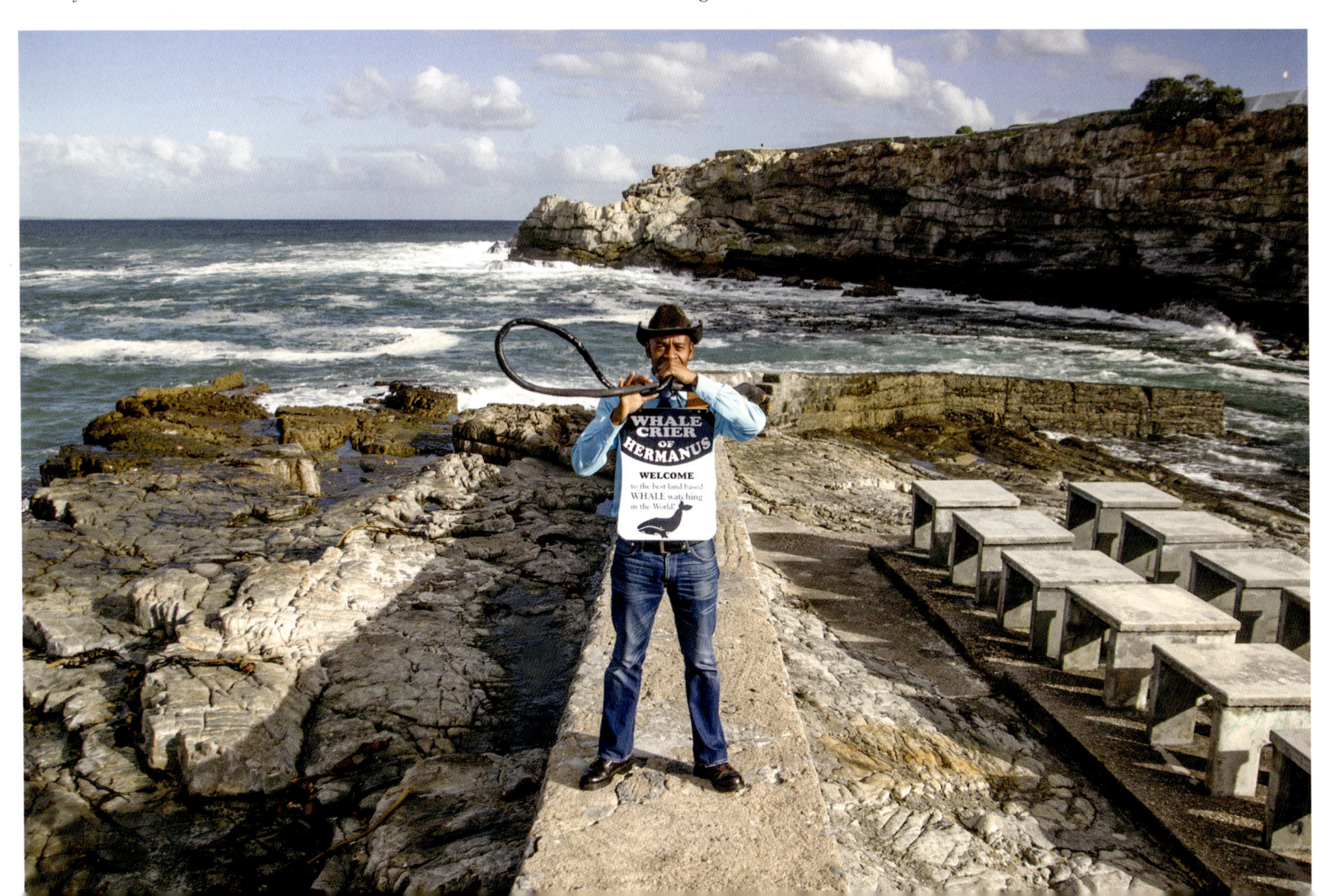

Whale-watching sites

'The Whale Walk has not only drawn attention to the conservation needs of cetaceans, but it has also shown how privileged we are to be able to stand on the rocks at the edge of the sea and spend time with these great ocean travellers.'

Noel Ashton, *A Quick Guide to the Whales of Southern Africa*, 2015

Whale-watching excursions by boat are popular. Three licensed whale-watching cruises operating in Hermanus depart daily from the New Harbour. One can also set out in a kayak from the Old Harbour or take to the skies with African Wings on a whale-viewing flight. Walking tours along the cliffs are popular as well. Whatever your choice of whale-watching activity, remember the watchword should always be: observe and do not disturb!

There are many places in the world where whales can be seen but few are as spectacular and convenient as the cliffs of Walker Bay. In order to enhance this experience, in 2006 marine environmentalist Noel Ashton partnered with the International Fund for Animal Welfare to launch the innovative Whale Walk, comprising informative whale and dolphin signboards positioned along the Cliff Path on the seafront.

A selection of the best whale-watching sites in Hermanus includes:

- the Old Harbour
- Gearing's Point, with its creative whale fluke seat and nature information boards
- Windsor Bay on Marine Drive
- just off Fick's Pool at Dreunkrans ('thundering cliff')
- just off the tidal pool at The Marine
- Kraal Rock, Sievers Point and Kwaaiwater
- beyond the surf at Voëlklip and Grotto Beach
- along the coast at Hawston and Vermont
- Onrus and Sandbaai.

Boat-based whale watching is one of the best ways of experiencing the wonder and mystery of whales in their natural environment.

WHALE-WATCHING TIPS

- Peak whale-watching season is September and October.
- Get a copy of a guide to whales.
- For shore-based viewing you'll need a good pair of binoculars, a camera with a 200-millimetre lens if you wish to take dramatic pictures, a hat, sunscreen lotion and plenty of patience.
- Keep safety in mind when you're on a cliff edge or on the rocks close to the breakers.
- Respect the property rights of others and the environment in general.
- For boat-based viewing you'll need the same basic items. Also take along a wide-angle lens in case of a really close encounter – and to record the reactions of fellow passengers. You'll have to take anti-nausea precautions if you're prone to seasickness.
- Make sure the skipper has the required permit, and follow his or her instructions.
- Clear, wind-free conditions are the best for viewing, but tend to lull whales into inactivity.
- Keep noise and activity levels down.
- Southern rights can be identified by the callosities on their heads and the absence of a dorsal fin.

Vic Cockroft and Peter Joyce, *Whale Watch: A Guide to Whales and Other Marine Mammals of Southern Africa*, 1998

Whale activities

The barrel-shaped body of a whale ends in an enormous tail, which provides the driving power for swimming and diving. It is believed these nautical giants evolved from large four-legged amphibians called anthracotheres some 60 million years ago, and have successfully adapted to a marine existence. The hippo is thought to be the closest living land relative of whales. Their daily activities, clearly visible from the various viewing points, include:

BREACHING

A whale can lift its entire body out of the water in a massive, graceful leap, falling back into the sea with an enormous splash. Keep watching when this happens, as they usually breach three to five times in succession. This is a spectacular sight. Scientists are not yet sure whether it is a means of communication, an aggressive display or simply an act of sheer exuberance. Some believe it may be a way of ridding themselves of the barnacles on their skin.

SPYHOPPING

Whales lift their heads and part of their bodies out of the water vertically. This gives them a 360-degree view of the world above the water.

LOBTAILING

Whales slap their tails on the surface, producing loud claps. This can be done repeatedly over long periods. It may be a form of social communication or a warning of rival whales or sharks.

SAILING

Whales sometimes lift their tails clear of the water for long periods. This could be a means of catching the wind to 'sail' through the water or a way of cooling down.

BLOWING

Whales make a hollow, echoing sound when air, accompanied by a spout of water, is expelled from the lungs through the blowhole. The shape of the spout enables whale watchers to identify the specific type of whale.

GRUNTING

Often heard at night, this loud, bellowing sound carries over a distance of up to two kilometres.

PLAYING WITH KELP

Whales seem to enjoy close contact with kelp, rubbing themselves, particularly their heads, against the long fronds. This could be a means of shedding loose skin caused by whale lice.

COMMUNICATION

Whales are acoustic creatures. Through sound, they take bearings, detect and avoid objects, find food and evade enemies. The sea is a vast echo chamber constantly bombarded with noise. A whale's sonar broadcast system is its most important item of survival equipment. Where the threshold of human hearing is between 30 and 16,000 Hertz (cycles per second), whales and dolphins can hear a range of frequencies from 100 to 150,000 Hertz.

THE SHARKS OF WALKER BAY

'Sharks are beautiful animals, and if you're lucky enough to see lots of them, that means that you're in a healthy ocean. You should be afraid if you are in the ocean and don't see sharks.'

Dr Sylvia Earle, oceanographer and conservationist

Cartilaginous fish such as sharks, skates and rays are collectively referred to as elasmobranchs, a word that derives from the Greek words *elasmos* and *brankhia*, meaning 'metal plate' and 'gills' respectively.

Elasmobranchs have some notable characteristics:
- The skeleton is made of cartilage rather than bone.
- They have five to seven gill openings on each side.
- They have rigid dorsal fins (and spines, if present).
- The upper jaw is not fused to the skull.
- Elasmobranchs have several rows of teeth which are continually replaced.

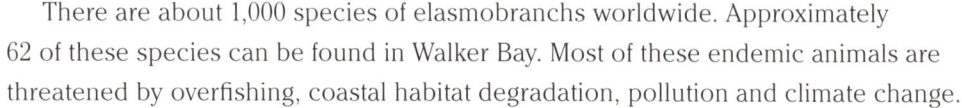

There are about 1,000 species of elasmobranchs worldwide. Approximately 62 of these species can be found in Walker Bay. Most of these endemic animals are threatened by overfishing, coastal habitat degradation, pollution and climate change.

Most sharks are fairly harmless, feeding on molluscs or plankton. Great white sharks, on the other hand, are one of a small number of shark species that prey on large marine mammals such as seals and whales.

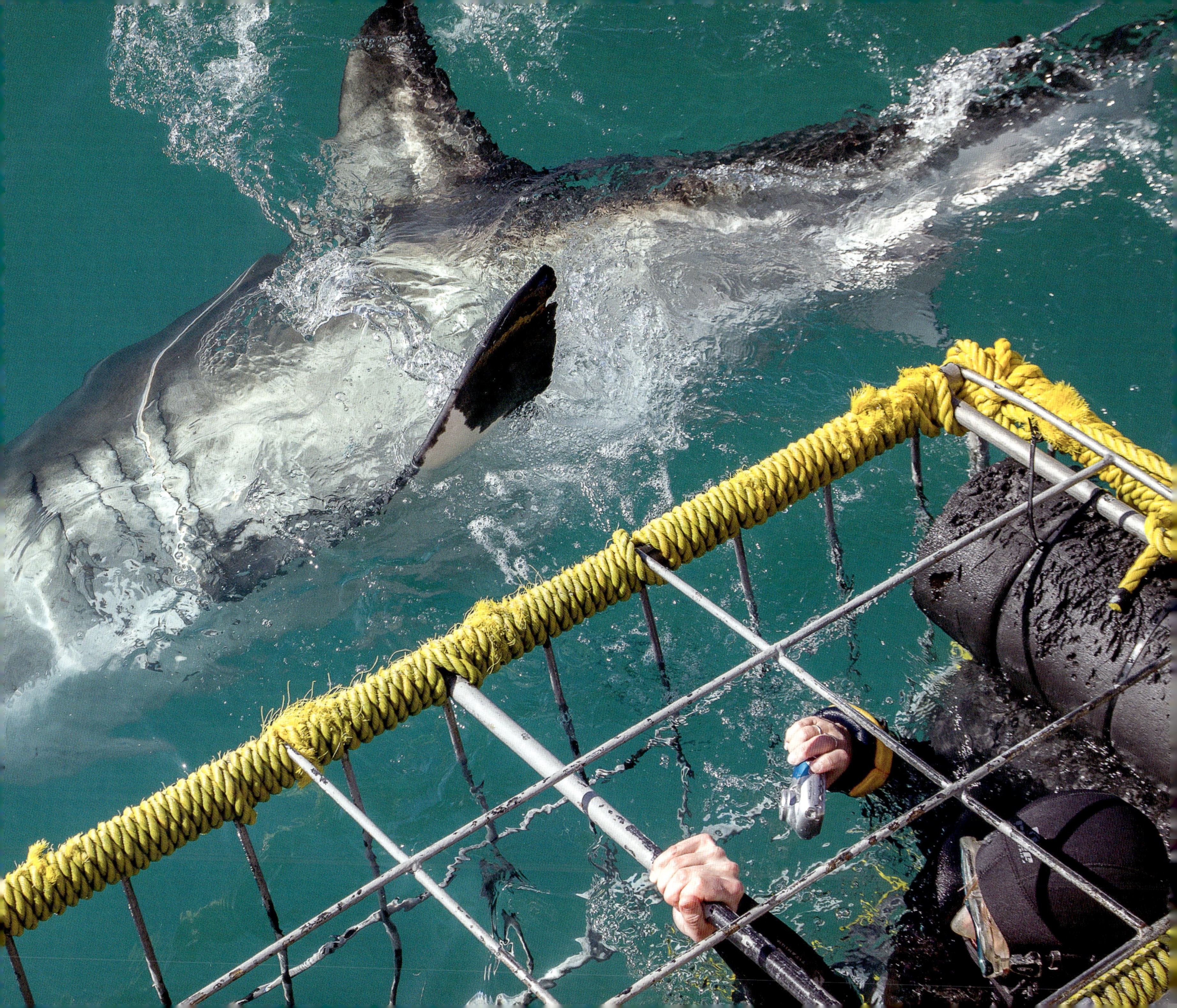

South African Shark Conservancy

'With every drop of water you drink, every breath you take, you're connected to the sea. No matter where on Earth you live.'

Dr Sylvia Earle, Mission Blue

Down a flight of steps at the Old Harbour, just below the cliffs where dassies peep at you from undercover ledges and the sea encircles a rocky outcrop, you will come to a rustic little building which accommodates the South African Shark Conservancy (SASC). Here, indoor experimental tanks with a flow-through saltwater system are the temporary home to some of the sharks that inhabit the waters of Walker Bay. At the SASC, over 2,000 individual sharks, representative of 27 species, have been tagged, providing valuable insight into their abundance and movement patterns in the area. At the conservancy there is also an education centre as well as a nursery where developing shark egg cases are incubated.

An excursion to the shark conservancy can be a fascinating and memorable experience. The tour includes 'shark bonding', where visitors are encouraged to stroke a shark, as well as a viewing of Baited Remote Underwater Video (BRUV) footage of an undersea world where marine creatures of all shapes and sizes co-exist, albeit not always peacefully. You may see a bugle-cheeked octopus take a sudden dive for cover when a stingray comes moseying along, or be entertained by a group of spindly-legged crayfish stalking the seabed like ballerinas with arthritis. A sevengill cowshark seems to take pleasure in banging the metal bait box and cable about with its jaws, swimming off and disappearing from the screen, only to reappear for the next round.

One shark with which you may share a special 'meet and greet' moment is the dark shyshark; if you stroke this marine animal you will notice that, although its white belly is smooth, its beautiful tapestry-patterned back has a grainy sandpaper texture. The shyshark earns its name from its tendency, when perceiving any threat, to curl into a doughnut and cover its eyes with its tail. The more extrovert leopard catshark, by contrast, enjoys engaging with people, and swims eagerly to the tank surface at feeding time. When threatened, it will also curl into a ring.

The shark conservancy was founded by Meaghen McCord in 2007. Meaghen has a BSc Honours degree in Marine Biology and an MSc in Fisheries Science. She is a member of the International

The leopard catshark has irregular black spots on the body and fins.

The South African Shark Conservancy's research efforts focus on sharks and their habitats. The dark shyshark, such as the one seen here, lives in shallow inshore areas, and can reach 60 centimetres when fully grown.

Union for Conservation of Nature (IUCN) Shark Specialist Group and has spent almost two decades working on various aspects of shark biology, ecology and management.

The interns who volunteer at the SASC do amazing work. One of their daily tasks is to drop bait boxes some 40 metres down to the seabed, and then lug them back up again after a day's work.

The focus of the SASC is to carry out important research and conservation work on commercially fished – and lesser known – shark, skate and ray species. The conservancy's cetacean research programme is focused on the monitoring of southern right whales and dolphins. In association with their commercial partner, Southern Right Charters, the SASC monitors the behaviour of these animals in Walker Bay. The techniques employed include photo-identification, behavioural coding and environmental monitoring.

In 2013 the SASC received the Overstrand Mayoral Environmental Award for Environmental Excellence. In 2014 it contributed to the declaration of the Cape Whale Coast Hope Spot, an initiative started by oceanographer and conservationist, Dr Sylvia Earle, under the banner of Mission Blue, an alliance of organisations established to increase the protection of the ocean. One of Mission Blue's goals is to educate and create awareness, in order to promote positive changes in the relationship between humans and marine life.

Meaghen McCord and her team are true blue heroes of the deep!

Shark cage diving

'Great whites are curious and investigative animals ... when they bite something unfamiliar to them ... they are looking for tactile evidence about what it is.'

Aidan Martin, Director, ReefQuest Centre
for Shark Research, Vancouver

White Shark Projects runs shark cage diving tours from Gansbaai.

An attraction that has made a quantum leap in popularity is shark cage diving. The purchase of a ticket will take you out on a boat as far as Dyer Island and Geyser Rock, where the largest and most powerful predatory fish in the sea feed off the abundant seal life. Shark Alley, between the two islands, is the best viewing site for the great white and the habitat of up to 50,000 Cape fur seals.

The cage-diving industry offers an adrenaline high in a wetsuit. Should you prefer not to enter the water, there is the option of remaining on deck to view the natural ecosystem of marine wildlife, including great whites, seals, dolphins, whales, African penguins and various seabird species.

Globally there are more than 450 species of shark, and about 100 of these are found in the waters off the South African coast.

The boats set off daily from a small harbour at Kleinbaai ('small bay'), near Gansbaai. It takes only 15 minutes to reach the favoured feeding grounds of the great white. Once the boat is anchored, the crew brief the passengers about the graceful, powerful and inquisitive creatures that cruise these waters.

The peak season for viewing sharks is from April to September, although they are seen all year round off the coast.

LOVE SHARKS, LOVE THE OCEAN

We must not only defend sharks because they are useful and beautiful, but we must protect the sea that feeds them. And also restore the balance of the great ocean's ecosystem, of which sharks form an important link and on which we ultimately depend.

Shark and Ray Project, Cousteau Society

Great white shark.

A steel cage is securely attached to the side of the tour operator's boat to give divers a close-up view of great white sharks, the ocean's apex predator.

Intrepid photographer Johann Kruger took up the challenge, and joined an excursion to capture some great shark shots from the deck. Here is his story:

'No matter how many documentaries you've watched, there is nothing like the moment when you see a great white shark for the first time effortlessly glide through perfectly calm water. You realise you are sitting on a little floating island in their environment, and you start to enter the water, separated from them only by the customised shark cage. Together with the pre-launch briefing, this is probably one of the most exciting experiential learning opportunities on Planet Earth: meeting one of the top predators face to face. White Shark Projects impressed me with their safety precautions, their commitment to shark research and involvement in the community. They are Fair Trade in Tourism South Africa certified. Several other reputable and experienced operators launch from the same facilities in Kleinbaai.'

HERMANUS

Shark protection

'For most of history, man has had to fight nature to survive; in this century he is beginning to realise that, in order to survive, he must protect it.'

Jacques-Yves Cousteau, scientist and oceanic explorer

Research shows that the South African white shark population is dwindling, and the species could be heading for extinction.

The importance of the great white shark cannot be overstated. Apart from the iconic status of these magnificent animals, they are apex predators, which means that they have no natural predators – other than humans. Their loss would have a detrimental effect on the ecological stability of the marine environment.

In 1991 South Africa became the first country to declare the great white a protected species. Subsequently many other countries have followed the same course, with a common goal: to preserve this apex predator. Since September 2004, great whites have been on the CITES List of Endangered Species. The latest CITES study reports that humans kill between 70 and 100 million sharks a year.

In South Africa, the most severe threats to sharks are trawlers, longliners, and anglers, along with the bather protection nets that have been operational along the KwaZulu-Natal coast since the 1960s. Other contributing factors are poaching, pollution, habitat encroachment and depletion of their food sources. Issues of future concern include continuing coastal development, global warming and pollution, as well as proposals to build new nuclear power plants close to delicate great white shark aggregation areas.

Shark facts

Satellite and radio-tagging data show that great whites make annual migrations, diving to depths of over 1,000 metres in the open ocean before heading for a coastal aggregation site.

A shark must keep moving in order to breathe. Most fish pump water over their gills when they are not moving, but many shark species need to swim through water with their gill slits open in order to create a flow across their gills. The great white shark is one such species.

A shark also needs to swim in order not to sink. Unlike other fish, sharks do not have a swimbladder, so they have no way of adjusting their buoyancy in water. Instead, they use their pectoral fins like the wings of an aeroplane to give them lift, in conjunction with continuous propulsion from the tail.

As partial endotherms, great whites can regulate the temperature of their core muscles and stomach considerably above that of the ambient seawater, which allows them to hunt effectively in cool, temperate environments.

Great whites have large, triangular, serrated teeth.

The eyesight of a shark is ten times more sensitive than our own in dim light, enabling them to spot prey clearly even in deep water. Sharks also detect prey by picking up electrical pulses.

They have a very keen sense of smell and are renowned for their ability to detect blood in water, picking it up from as far as 500 metres away. On impact with its prey, a great white rolls its eyes back in its head for protection.

Most sharks are predators that feed by slicing chunks off their prey or swallowing it whole. They do not chew; most species have extremely acidic digestive juices, which can dissolve bone.

Their teeth have sharp serrated edges, adapted to cutting through their prey rather than holding onto it. A shark may have more than 100 teeth in its mouth at one time – quite a jawful – but this is because they continually grow, lose and replace their teeth. In fact, a shark may go through as many as 20,000 teeth in a long lifetime.

The great white has a lifespan of 70 years and more. The male can reach between six and nine metres in length. Females grow even larger than the males, and can weigh more than three tons.

Females give birth to an average of eight or nine fully formed young, each measuring about 1.5 metres in length. Unlike whales, which raise their young, shark pups leave the mother immediately after birth, seeking sheltered areas where there is a plentiful supply of food, as well as refuge from other predators.

SIX SENSES

Sharks have a battery of finely tuned senses at their disposal to help them find prey. They usually first detect food from a distance by sound or smell. At closer range, they use eyesight and the ability to detect the electrical pulses given off by a creature. They may use taste-bud clusters in their mouths to analyse a 'test bite'. Like most fish, sharks also have a lateral line that detects changes in water pressure.

Daniel Gilpin, *The Mighty Oceans*, 2006

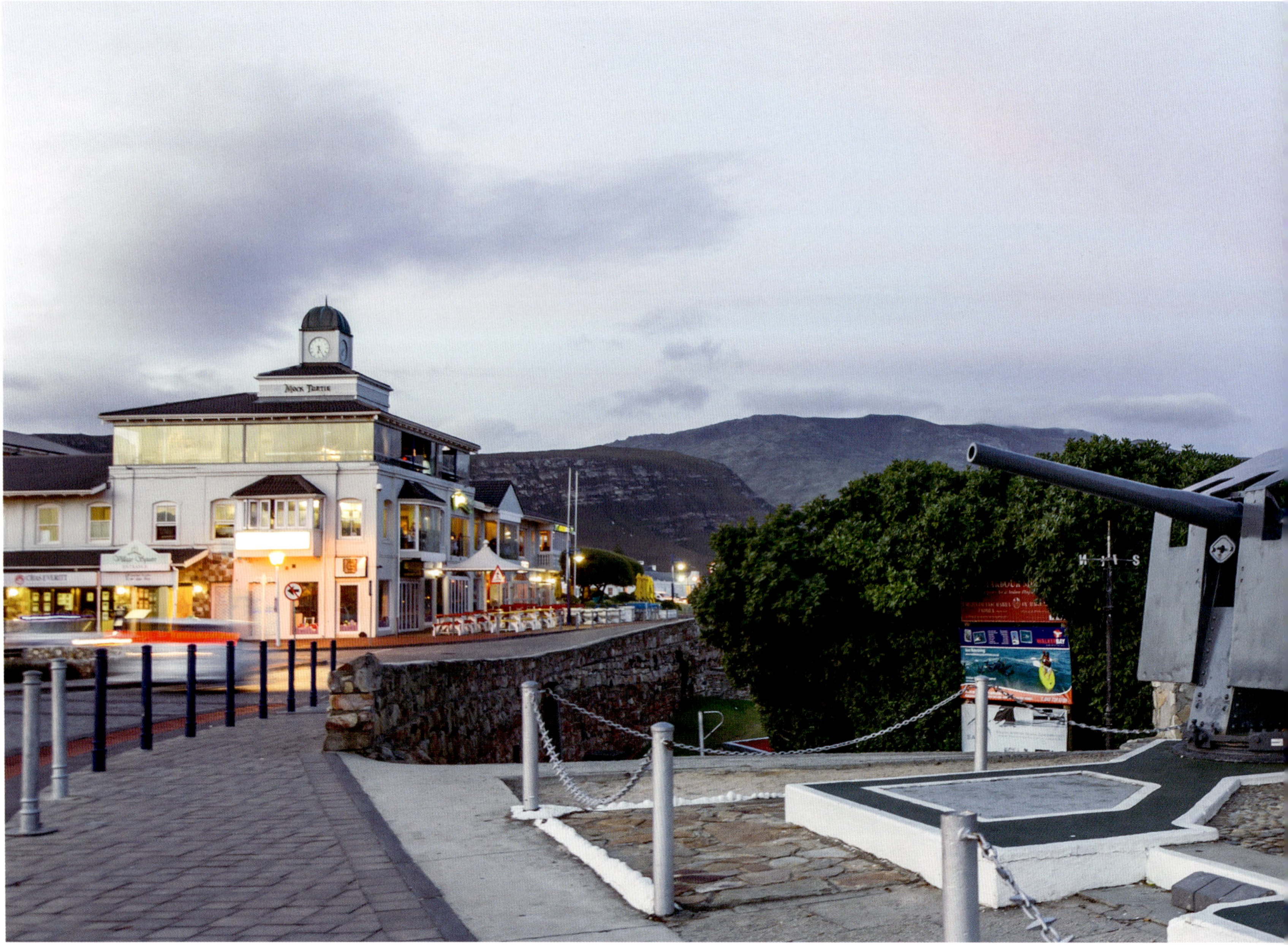

THE TOWN CENTRE – HEART OF HERMANUS

'Progress is impossible without change, and those who cannot change their minds cannot change anything.'

George Bernard Shaw, Irish playwright

The changing tides of time have taken Hermanus from a modest fishing village to a town riding the swells of development and commerce, along with a growing residential population. The heritage of the original village has been retained in a number of renovated fishermen's cottages, some which have been converted into shops, offices and restaurants. The structure of the Old Town centre remains compact, and most amenities are within walking distance.

A beautiful historical feature of Hermanus is the church for the patron saint of fishermen, St Peter's, located on Main Road. The old stone building, constructed in 1868, is graced by a shady garden – a sanctuary amid a busy retail precinct.

The Village Square, home to an eclectic mix of restaurants and retail shops, looks out over the Old Harbour and the Hermanus War Memorial (left). The monument was erected in 1929 in memory of 11 soldiers from Hermanus who died in World War I. The names of another 15 soldiers were added after World War II. Within walking distance is the Church of St Peter (above).

HERMANUS 81

The Village Square with its clock tower is a distinctive landmark situated close to the Old Harbour. A short distance from the town centre, this locale is the hub of the tourist industry. In its stylish two-level arcade, exclusive speciality shops intermingle with a mix of restaurants spilling out onto the paved square. The waterfront piazza provides a perfect setting for dining alfresco against the backdrop of a sculpted whale-fluke fountain, while having fun spotting the real thing in the bay. A more recent addition to the square is a raised walk-on chessboard where you can make your move while perusing the menu. Entertainment is on offer in a terraced outdoor amphitheatre rolling down to the Cliff Path and Old Harbour.

In contrast to the Village Square's fashionable interiors, the Market Square, situated next door, is home to a vibrant mini mall of outdoor stalls. Here the emphasis is on locally produced wares as well as products from across South Africa. The vision of this market is to create opportunities for local entrepreneurs specialising in a variety of crafts and trades – from clothing and accessories to jewellery and curios; from home-made goodies and smoothies to biltong and braai accessories; from arts and crafts to the Photo Shed, where spectacular visual images of the region are exhibited.

Another drawcard for visitors is the range of stalls that promote a variety of marine excursions: here you can make

Aside from exquisite views across Walker Bay, the Old Town's attractions and entertainment come in many forms: a walk-on chessboard at the Village Square (opposite, above left), cocktails on the terrace of the Harbour House hotel (above centre), a sculptural masterpiece, *Sea Change* by Anton Smit, that is also a signpost (above right) opposite the Burgundy Restaurant, and the colourful crafts on Market Square (left).

84 HERMANUS

bookings for a Playa Cruise – with its promise of experiencing an amazing sunset over Walker Bay while sipping a glass of chilled champagne on deck – or you can purchase tickets to join an adventure cruise or go snorkelling or diving with mako sharks. In addition, the ticket office and departure point of Hermanus Wine Hoppers, which offers unique hop-on hop-off safari-style wine tours, is located in this hub. With its lively vibe, this market is definitely worth a visit.

A satellite office of the Hermanus Tourism Bureau is also conveniently positioned at Market Square to guide you from A to Z on your travels in the Overberg.

The heart of the Old Town entices you down memory lane with a visit to a mix of nostalgic shops, adding their own brand of charm to the Hermanus central business district. Welcoming you in Main Road, directly opposite St Peter's Church, is Niel du Toit's *Algemene Handelaar*. This bona fide general dealer is a fabulous old-fashioned store; with its bulky wooden and glass counters, it is truly redolent of yesteryear and typically displays a wide variety of goods. There's kitchenware, stationery, hardware, toys, picture framing and a gardening department. Down the aisle, past rows of bottles of benzine, methylated spirits and turpentine, you are likely to find whatever it is you are looking for, from a bathroom plug to a gas stove. You can even purchase sweets here – the old-fashioned kind – and engage with the owner himself. Niel du Toit is a young octogenarian whose father started the business in the late 1940s. In those days, food produce and draperies were sold at the shop. Niel took over the family business in February 1958 and introduced self-service. He has been there ever since, demonstrating his staying power through changing times.

Spiros Jewellers, located on the corner of Main Road, is a family-owned business. This timeless jewel in the crown of the Old Town is under the proprietorship of Andrew Paizes. Back in the day, when Hermanus was still a village, Andrew's father-in-law, Spiros Maroudas, a Greek immigrant, opened his shop in the seaside town.

A colourful assortment of shops (top) and the Honey Stall (opposite, bottom centre) can be found in the heart of Hermanus. Familiar faces in this district include Niel du Toit, the general dealer (opposite, bottom left), and Andrew Paizes, proprietor of Spiros Jewellers (left).

HERMANUS 85

Visiting Romantiques is to step straight into the past. All manner of vintage items from different eras, whether the 1960s (top left) or the 1940s (above), are for sale here. It even has a vintage cinema (top right).

The establishment's quaint interior, with its old-fashioned fittings, evokes a sense of the past. Steeped in the skills of craftsmanship, Spiros specialises in general jewellery and repairs. His family home on Gearing's Point, once the original homestead of Sidney Gearing, a former mayor, is today a well-known heritage site and the only remaining house standing on that part of Marine Drive.

Nostalgia is what makes Romantiques tick. Although only a decade or so old, it's a fascinating shop, and one where time seems to go backwards. Where in an antique emporium, or any other place for that matter, could you find a small period-piece 'bioscope' with its own box office, rows of authentic cinema chairs, a movie screen artistically framed by red velvet stage drapes, and vintage posters adorning the walls? The projector, with its genuine 16-millimetre reel-to-reel films, offers a cinematic range of enduring movies starring unforgettable names like Charlie Chaplin, Bette Davis, Laurence Olivier, Ava Gardner and many more. Attending the Movie-Go-Round Saturday matinee at this vintage theatre is a

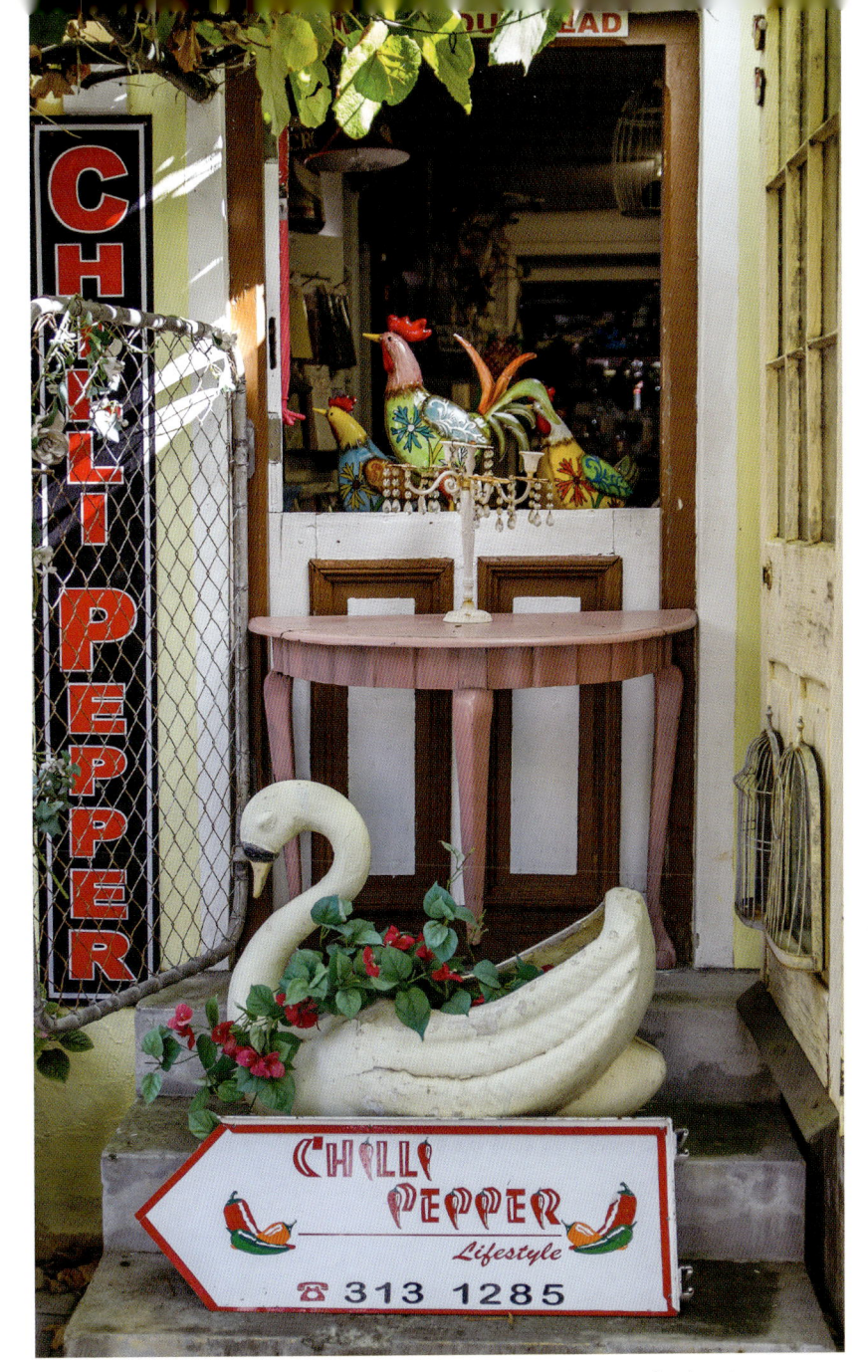

Chilli Pepper's lane gives a sneak preview of the riches inside the shop.

time-warp experience. After entering through a foyer, which is decked out in Coke memorabilia and Laurel and Hardy figurines, you may be transported straight into the magical atmosphere of a slapstick silent short, starring Harold Lloyd, that will have the audience packing up with laughter. Then comes the main feature, perhaps set in the early twentieth century. Amazing entertainment steeped in the 'good old days' will have you spellbound. Viva the romance of Movie-Go-Round – pass the popcorn!

Romantiques is a treasure trove of bygones and collectables – such as Grandmother's rolling pin and antiquated gadgets that come with buttons and knobs but don't need electricity – a vintage clothing department with life-sized mannequins, and a phenomenal range of militaria, porcelain, toys, glassware, brass, nautical instruments … well, really, you name it and it's here. And in keeping with their pre-technological ethos, Romantiques has an old-fashioned push-button cash register, and transactions are strictly cash. Ching-ching … it's a classic!

A shop with a charm all of its own is Chilli Pepper, situated in Mitchell Street. You may spot the Harley Davidson or the Pontiac parked outside, and during the festive season a life-sized Santa stands beside a bubble box on the sidewalk blowing thousands of bubbles into the air. Step inside, where André Wolfswinkel and his wife, Theresa, have created a visual feast of beautiful artefacts, both retro and vintage. The allure of this shop extends to a leafy vine-covered lane to which the creative couple have added their artistic touch. It is perhaps not surprising that Chilli Pepper, with its enviable collection of memorabilia, also houses a fancy-dress section. The atmosphere within its walls makes a visit to this shop a magical Harry Potter experience.

HERMANUS 87

Left: Owned by actress Hélène Truter and her husband, Percy, Amulet is all about turning ordinary spaces into beautiful interiors. While Hélène's forte is the art of making things pretty, Percy is renowned for his carrot cake – a work of art in itself.

Opposite: David Lowe and Colleen Thonissen of Funky Vibes, displaying their characteristic brand of style.

On the same retail block is a pretty painted shop promising 'lifestyle in a room'. The owners of Amulet are Hélène Truter, a South African television celebrity, and her husband, Percy. They have brought the élan of beauty and joy into this arty-crafty shop, with its fusion of music and an outdoor water feature set in a quaint little alley. The French Provençal interior offers a sensual feast of fabric flowers, art, ceramics, clothing and gifts. Notice the whimsical touch of a tree-branch roof beam, from which porcelain cups are suspended with ribbons, and other quirky features added by this über-creative couple. Amulet is a speciality shop with lots of heart, and one whose owners have crafted it with love. In Hélène's own words: 'If you don't like it, tie a ribbon round it and make it pretty!' She has certainly mastered the art in this department. With freshly brewed coffee and Percy's famous carrot cake on offer, an Amulet interlude is guaranteed to lift the spirit and nourish the soul.

Louis Armstrong's famous lyric 'It don't mean a thing if it ain't got that swing' certainly does not apply to Funky Vibes, with its super-duper collection of music. An eclectic couple, David Lowe

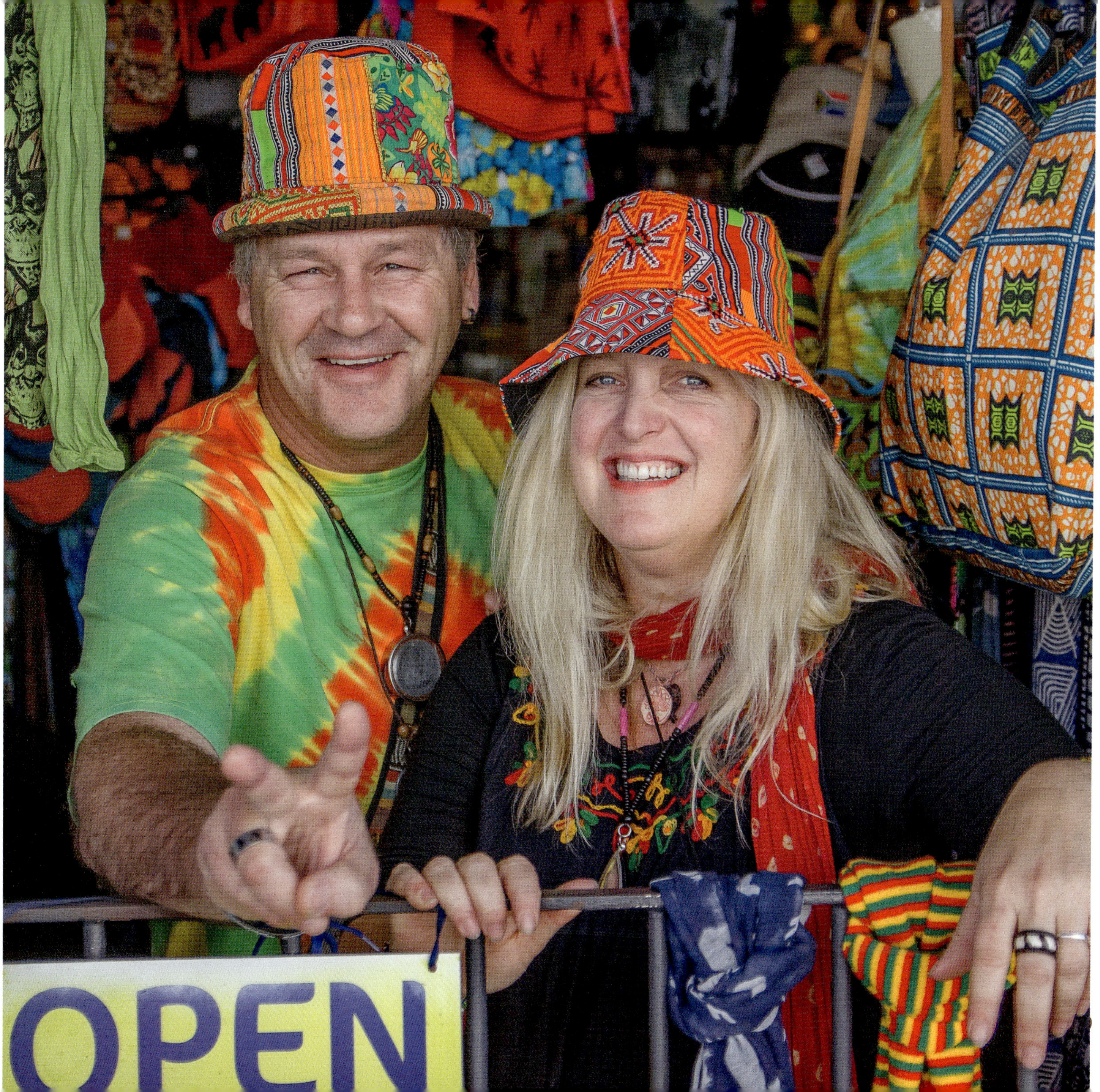
OPEN

Left: Beth and Noel Hunt lovingly created the literature experience that is today Hemingways of Harbour Road. Since opening its doors in 1995, the shop has built up a clientele of book lovers from all over the world.

Opposite left: John Morris of Book Cottage, located in Long Street, offers not only an impressive selection of books but also an array of classical music CDs.

Opposite right: Corinne Hendry, owner of Bookmark, has created a contemporary, light-filled environment for bibliophiles. The double-storey book-lover's paradise is in Main Road, close to The Marine.

Pages 92–93: Hermanus has a plethora of restaurants, cafés and coffee shops, making it an epicure's delight.

and Colleen Thonissen, apart from creating good vibrations on the airwaves, bring loads of colour to this fascinating shop with all kinds of interesting knick-knacks and their trademark range of imported and exotic clothing.

This cluster of quaint shops defines the Old Town of Hermanus. In the same league, a literary landmark that draws you in is Hemingways of Harbour Road − a bookshop filled with books whose authors have stood the test of time. Noel and I opened Hemingways in 1995, the centenary year of the iconic writer's birth. The shop is artistically laid out with antique bookshelves and memorabilia, and in each nook and cranny you will find something to rest your eye on while dipping into the printed page.

Hemingways has made its own mark in literature: South African author Rudie van Rensburg, in his novel *Judaskus*, writes about his eccentric veteran detective and hero who visits Hemingways to look at rare books on stamp collecting. In 2013 Hemingways was featured in Louis Vuitton's *Cape Town City Guide*, where it was favourably compared with Shakespeare and Company, the famous bookstore on Paris's Left Bank.

Lingering with literature but moving on in time, a new chapter has opened for Book Cottage, a well-established bookshop in town. Once a landmark in Harbour Road, Book Cottage has since relocated to Long Street under the proprietorship of John Morris. With his artistic flair and passion for the classics, John has added a valuable dimension to the cultural arts by incorporating an impressive well-stocked music room where you can sit and relax, browse through books and even have a game of chess while enjoying a cup of coffee.

Bookmark, another firm favourite, formerly situated in the East Cliff Centre, has found a cosy, new niche on Main Road, near The Marine hotel. Passionate bibliophile and owner Corinne Hendry has created an inviting upstairs-downstairs space to house a diverse range of expertly selected books.

Corinne hails from Edinburgh and, in true patriotic style, a Scottie dog clock adorns the wall of her delightful shop! A famous visitor to Corinne's bookshop was fellow Scot Ian Rankin, best-selling author of the popular Inspector Rebus detective novels set in Edinburgh.

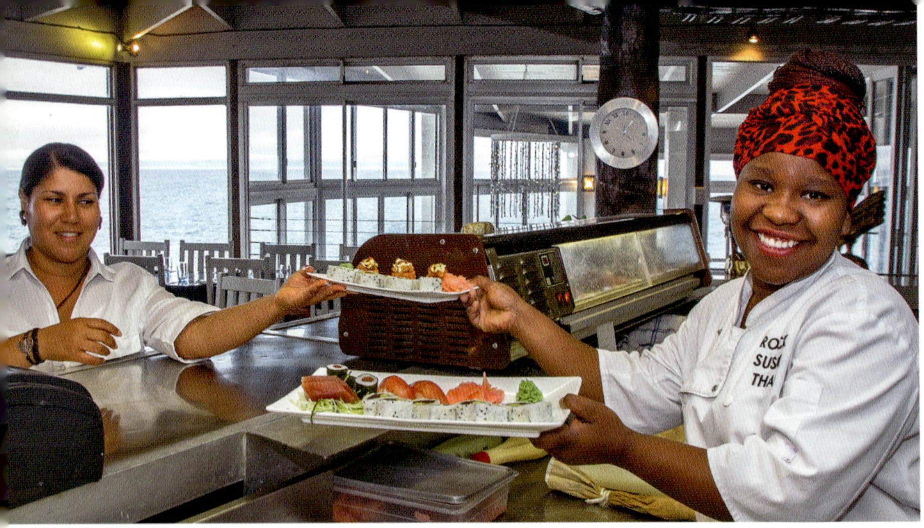

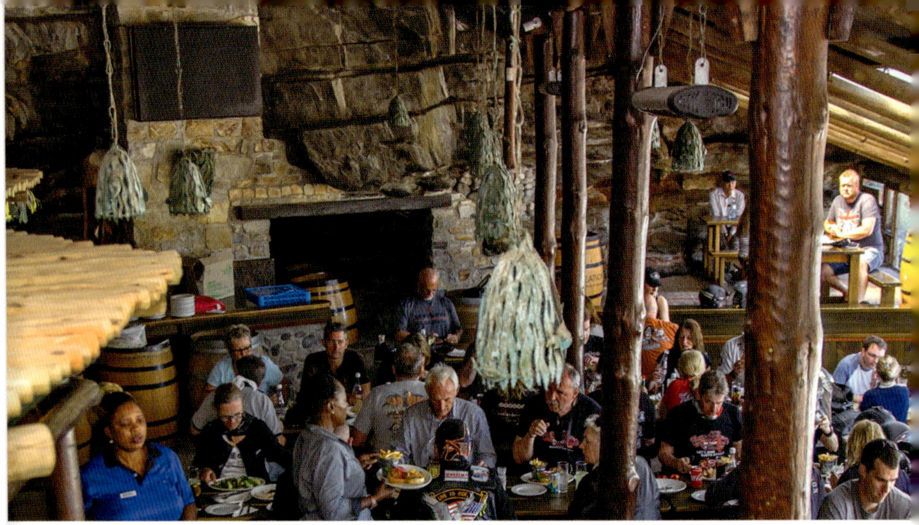

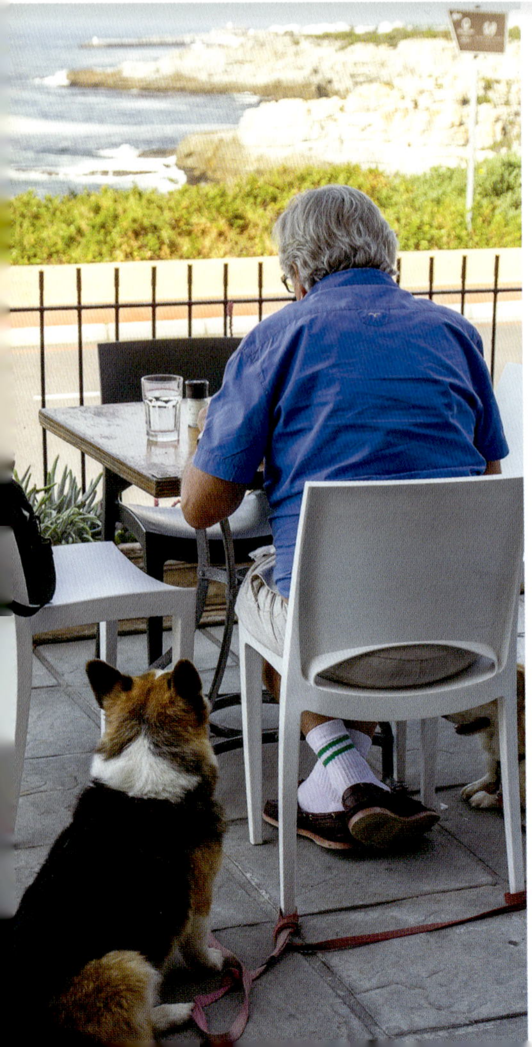

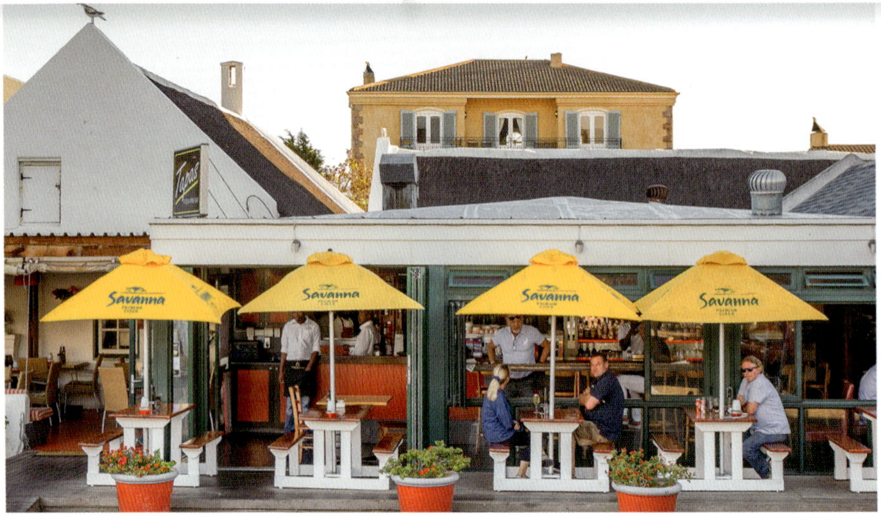
Savanna
Savanna
Savanna
Savanna

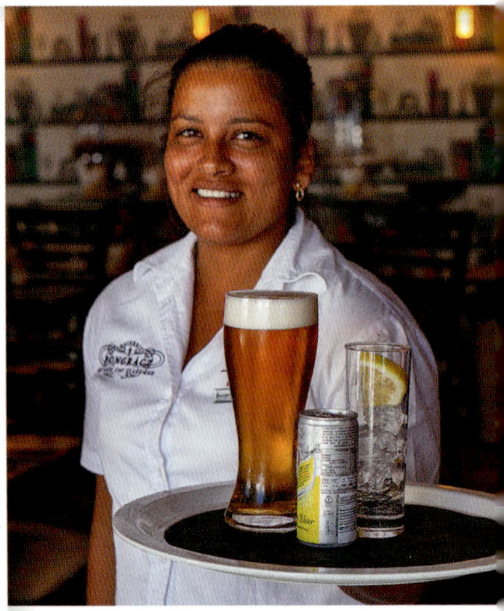

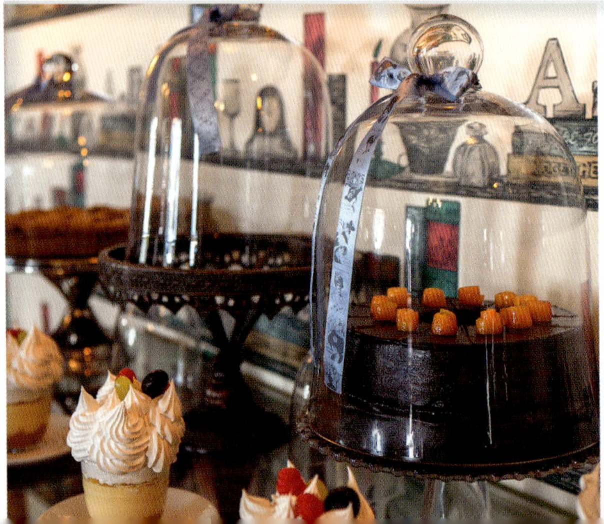

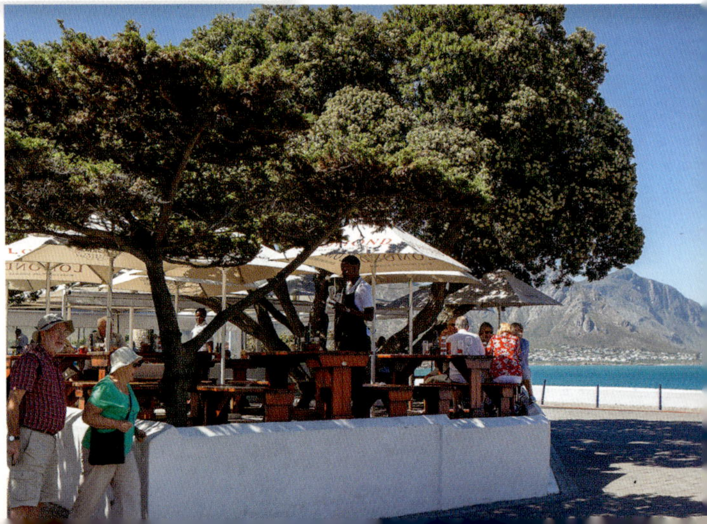

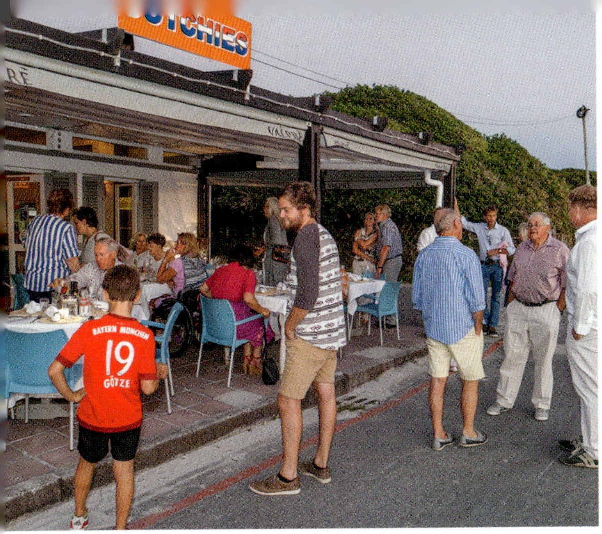
19
GÖTZE

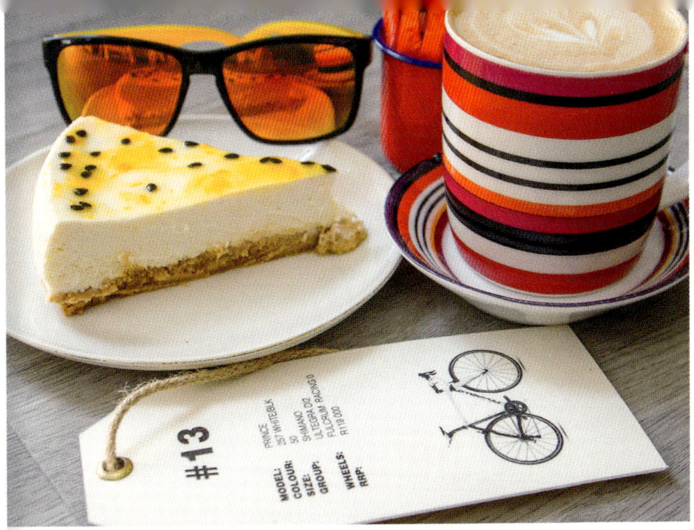
#13

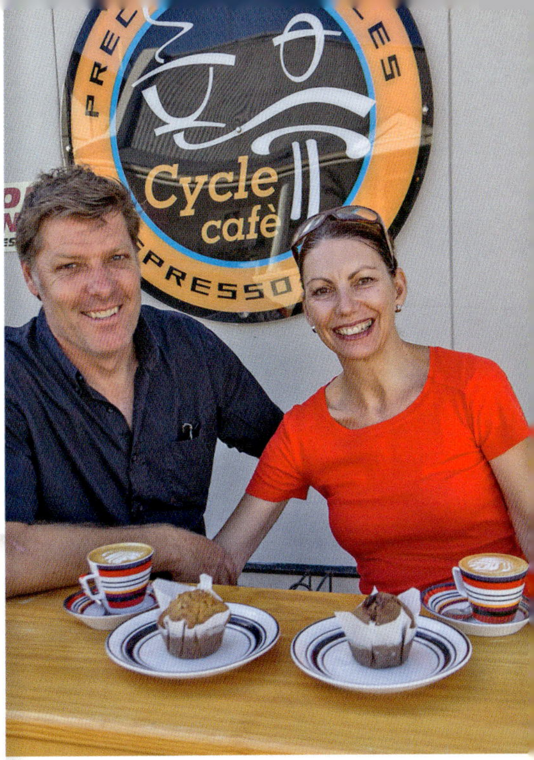
Cycle
café

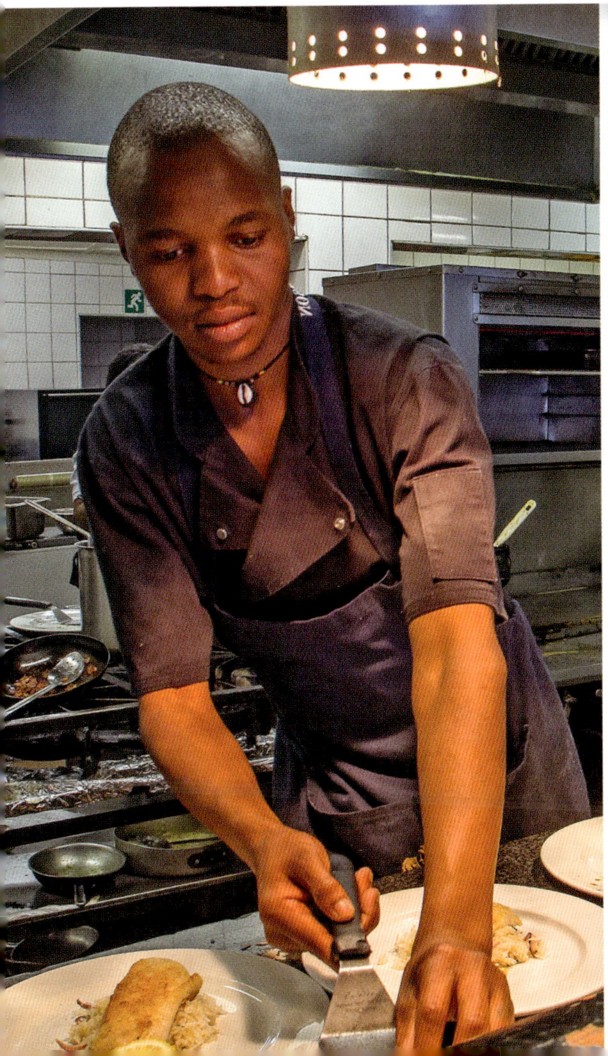

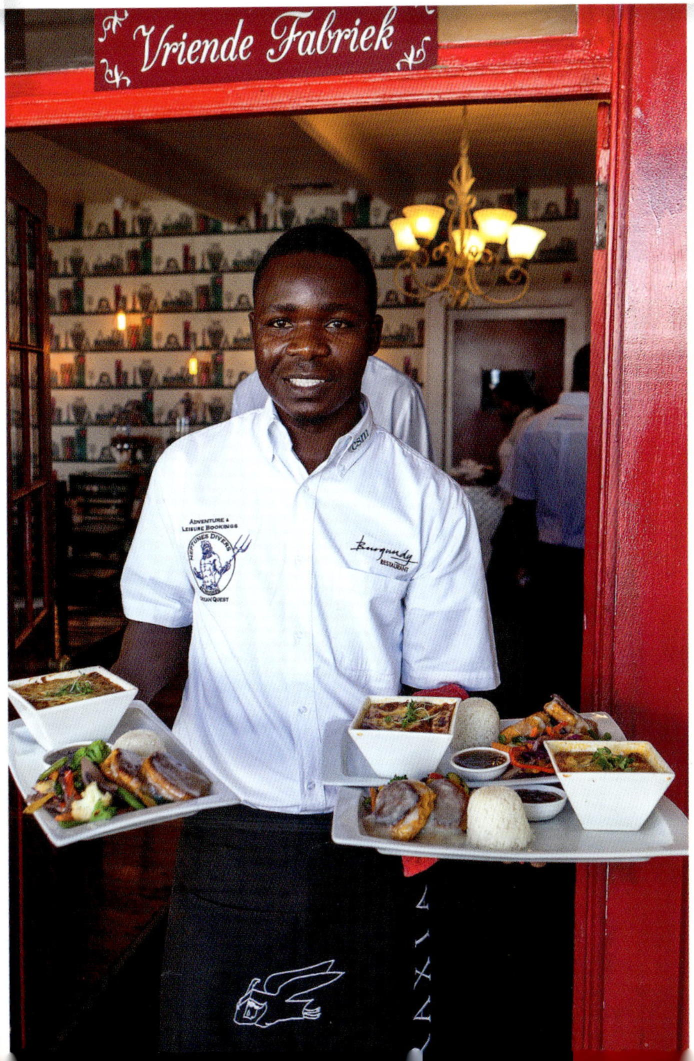
Vriende Fabriek

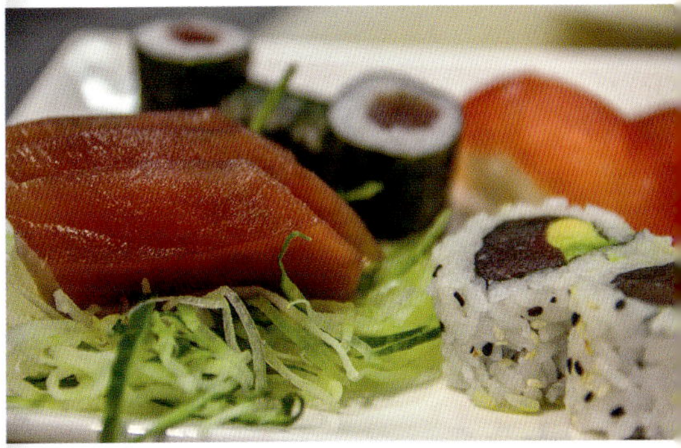

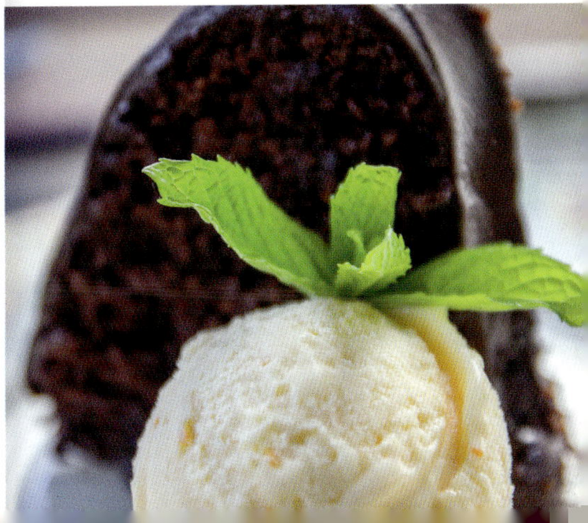

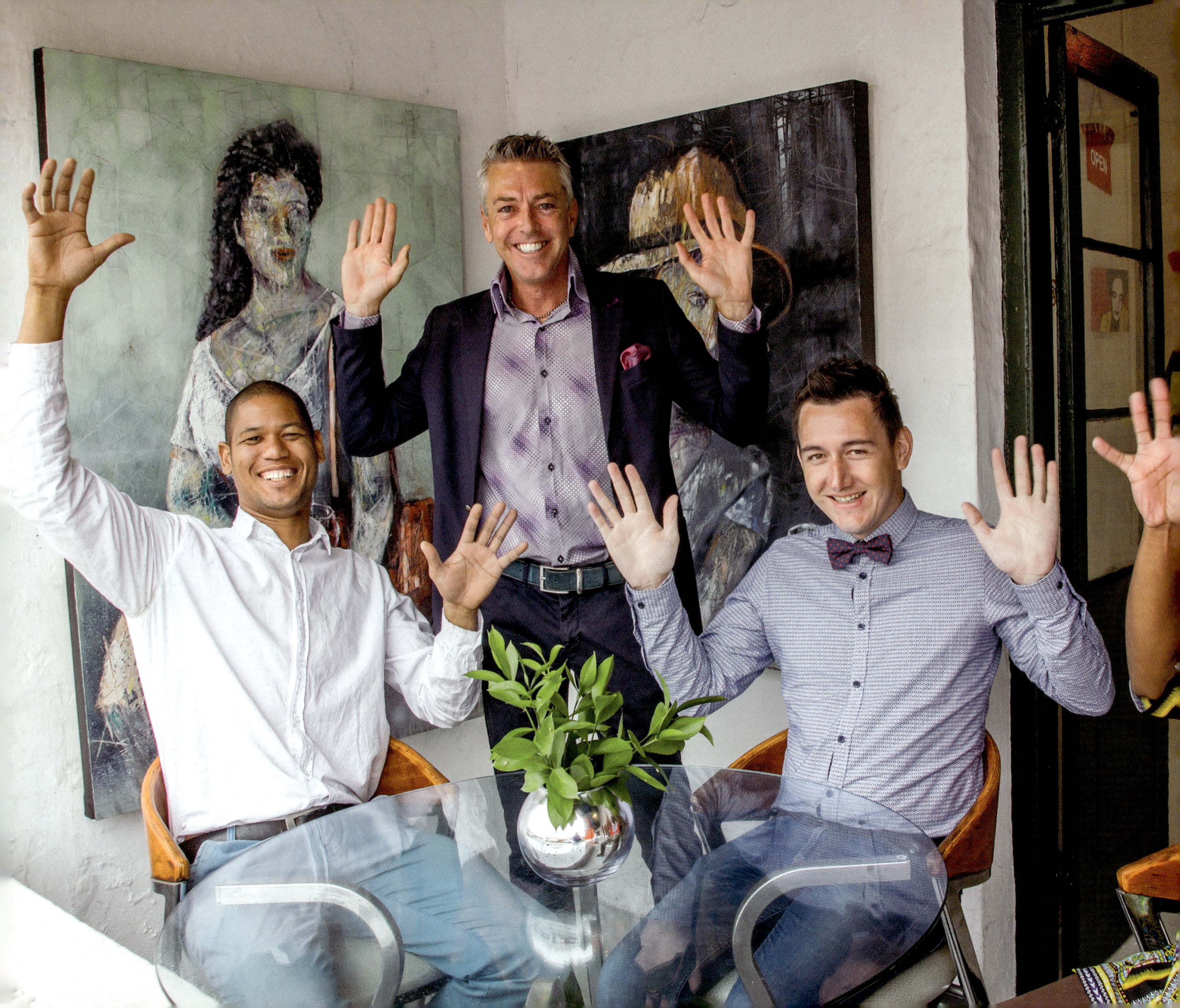
OPEN

CULTURAL HIGHLIGHTS

'South African art is experiencing a prime period in which we are increasingly becoming part of the international mainstream of contemporary art. We are making our mark of quality with confidence.'

Amanda Botha, journalist, documentary
film director and author of publications on art

Hermanus is a masterpiece! In summer, in a scene akin to that of the Mediterranean, the Overberg canvas is splashed with vibrant blue skies and an ocean rinsed in turquoise hues topped with white-crested waves. In winter, the surrounding lush countryside explodes into a profusion of dazzling yellow canola fields, reflecting a luminous light with radiant rainbows and captivating cloudscapes. Even a grey day at this seaside town has its own particular brand of beauty.

Hermanus, shaped by the elements of nature – its vivid colours and expressive landscapes – and a natural creative energy, has for years been a hub of artistic expression, a port of call for artists and other creative spirits from all walks of life: crafters, ceramicists, sculptors, photographers, writers, and those whose passion is the easel. Much of the artists' works can be seen in the many galleries in the town centre, a phenomenal artspace that has seen an explosion of exhibition events and studios in recent times.

Boosted by a thriving arts scene and a host of creative and cultural events and festivals throughout the year, Hermanus has become a choice destination for all those interested in aesthetics.

Jozua Rossouw (second from left) and his team at Rossouw Modern. This art gallery in Harbour Road showcases works from both emerging and established artists.

96 HERMANUS

First Fridays Artwalk

'Hermanus is the Art Destination of the Western Cape.'

Patrick Chapman, art columnist

Discover the pleasure of art with an evening amble through the many art galleries in Hermanus. First Fridays Artwalk, apart from being a monthly celebration of the town's wealth of artists, is part of a global initiative to bring art and art appreciation to the attention of the public.

'Artwalkers' have the opportunity of enjoying a cultural and social platform where people from all walks of life can come together in the spirit of artistic appreciation. During the evening, each gallery, decked in the Artwalk's orange emblem of Chinese lanterns and bunting while still exhibiting its own unique style and character, welcomes you with convivial hospitality and a glass of wine from the local vineyards.

The Artwalk also offers the opportunity of meeting and talking to some of the artists and gallery owners in an informal and relaxed atmosphere.

Opposite (clockwise, left to right): Artists at work – Charmaine de Jongh Gelderblom, Leon Müller, Malcolm Bowling and Ed Bredenkamp.

Above right: The owner of Lembu Gallery, Ian Macdonald (left), with internationally acclaimed ceramacist Catherine Brennon (seated) and fine art photographer Lawrance Brennon (right).

Right: Browsing at Lembu on First Fridays.

'Follow the orange' from one gallery to another and discover the wall-to-wall wonders of art. Whatever your taste, this visual experience gives you an entrée into a diversity of art forms and creative works, ranging from Old Masters to contemporary works, including ceramics, sculptures, paintings, fine crafts and jewellery.

Diarise this highlight, bearing in mind that the Artwalk goes into hibernation during the out-of-season winter months of June and July.

A map of the Artwalk route is obtainable from all participating galleries, including:

- Originals Art Gallery
- Lembu Gallery
- Rossouw Modern
- Forty x 40 Gallery
- Malcolm Bowling Art
- Rossouw Modern SPACE
- Abalone Gallery
- Bellini Gallery
- The Art Gallery
- Pure South
- Walker Bay Art Gallery
- Charmaine De Jongh Gelderblom Gallery
- Gallery 19
- Art Thirst
- Kunskantoor
- Canvas of Life

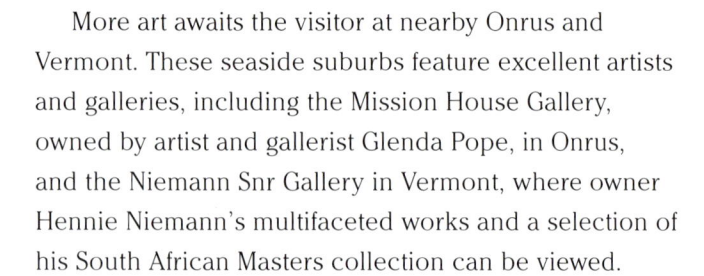

More art awaits the visitor at nearby Onrus and Vermont. These seaside suburbs feature excellent artists and galleries, including the Mission House Gallery, owned by artist and gallerist Glenda Pope, in Onrus, and the Niemann Snr Gallery in Vermont, where owner Hennie Niemann's multifaceted works and a selection of his South African Masters collection can be viewed.

Viva the art scene in Hermanus, our Montmartre of the Overberg!

There is a buzz on the streets on First Fridays as locals and visitors alike explore the town's art galleries and other exhibition spaces on foot.

Hermanus FynArts

'FynArts is a festival to celebrate the "finer" things in life – not for connoisseurs only, but also for ordinary people like us who are interested in, and would like to learn more about the arts.'

Mary Faure, founder Hermanus FynArts

Each year, during the month of June, Hermanus FynArts, a celebration of South African arts, creates an impressive programme of innovative and creative events, driven by passion and dedication.

Over a ten-day period, the town becomes a desirable destination for art aficionados and those who delight in gourmet cuisine, noble wines and the performing arts. Under the umbrella of Hermanus FynArts, you will find a fusion of workshops, talks, entertainment, food and wine, films, exhibitions, demonstrations and fun for children.

The quality of the FynArts festival and the hospitality of Hermanus make this a unique and memorable experience. This winter festival, held in the whale capital of the world, is an event not to be missed.

Hermanus FynArts is a signature arts festival and a splendid treat for all culture vultures!

The year-long Sculpture in the Cliffs exhibition is a flagship event of the annual FynArts festival. Works featured during 2016/2017 included *Love Alone* by George Holloway (top) and *Ouma Sarah* by Jean Theron Louw (above).

HERMANUS 99

HERMANUS

Markets, fairs and events

'It makes me so happy to see the same faces each week smiling, relaxing and enjoying what there is on offer, as these locals are what make this market so enjoyable for our tourists and visitors from out of town.'

Liza van Coppenhagen, Hermanus Country Market

Markets are a pleasant alternative to shopping malls in South Africa. When the weather is good, browsing through the stalls at an outdoor market is a relaxing, community-friendly experience; and pets are usually welcome too. Visitors can stroll around the stalls at their own pace, stopping to admire or purchase a crafter's wares, while enjoying the festive atmosphere, a trademark of these events.

In this neck of the woods, markets have sprung up like mushrooms. One of the most popular, the Hermanus Country Market, is located at the cricket club, in a maze of rustic stalls beneath the trees. Saturday is market day, and this venue is

Food stalls offering a variety of delicious goodies – from organic produce and deli treats to wholesome takeaway lunches – are plentiful at the Hermanus Country Market.

that special place where you can meet for pleasure and leisure, slow down and partake of the Overberg's bread basket, overflowing with an abundant harvest of fresh produce, individual chef specialities, and handcrafted wines and beers. Live music, good coffee and scrumptious alfresco breakfasts – perhaps stretching to a leisurely midday lunch – certainly make this a market not to be missed. The organisers and market traders abide by the following motto: 'We love what we do and we try as best we can to run the market according to eco-friendly principles, and we are committed to creating a wholesome experience with a minimal impact on the environment.'

From one stall to another, creative talent abounds – as markets go, it doesn't get much better than this!

During the summer months, a Wednesday evening market is held at the same venue.

Another country-style place for a rendezvous, where you can wind down and enjoy a mellow Saturday morning, is the courtyard of the Hermanuspietersfontein Food and Wine Market. Steeped in the historical roots of the founder of the town, Hermanuspietersfontein is situated close to the Hemel-en-Aarde Village. Here, the marketers display their wares in an artistic wine cellar setting. Storyboards adorn the walls with culinary quotes, a reminder that no one needs to go hungry or thirsty here! On offer is a traditional regional *kos en wyn mark* (food and wine market) with delicious breakfasts and foodie fare ranging from cured meats, olives and cheeses to freshly shucked oysters and a variety of seafood delicacies, and much more. Help yourself from a buffet of the best and sit at outdoor tables beneath brollies while the kids enjoy the children's playpen close by.

Hermanus's diverse markets offer something for everyone. The Hermanuspietersfontein Food and Wine Market (left) attracts food lovers from far and wide, while the Sunday market at Lemm's Corner (above) features high-quality arts and crafts.

With live music to boot, this market is a show stopper. An added bonus is free wine tasting, with a variety of the cellar's wines available for purchase.

A true community garden market is to be found in the shady grounds of St Peter's Church. Each Saturday, traders bring their art and crafts, bric-a-brac, delicious home-bakes and other culinary goodies to town. At tables set out beneath the trees you can also enjoy the coffee morning, a successful and well-established church institution for many years. This market is located in the heart of the Old Town, and just a stone's throw from the sea. The traders' slogan puts it in a nutshell: 'A village market in a garden creating your lifestyle experience.'

Last but by no means least, the historic Lemm's Corner Market has made a welcome comeback after the absence of its once legendary craft market. This Sunday market offers a variety of crafts, art, slow food, craft beers and a wine bar. On occasion there is live music as well. Strolling through Lemm's Corner Market is a great way to enjoy a leisurely Sunday. The market is also open during the monthly First Fridays Artwalk.

A weekly visit to an outdoor market, offering arts and crafts created from the heart and food made with love, makes for a truly *local is lekker* experience.

A local hat maker adds fun and colour to the market at Lemm's Corner.

MARKET DAY

Saturday mornings make for a weekly pilgrimage to the market. The 'dorp' inhabitants are spoilt for choice with practically a market in every direction. Each has its own charm and character and what you can't find at one you can probably find at another. But whatever the shopping style, baskets are soon filled with a variety of goodies – freshly picked tomatoes, farm bread, home-made mustard, a bunch of lavender, lemon syrup, and the list goes on ...

Glenda Furst, Market Mengelmoes, from *Hermanus Cooks*, 2009

Hermanus Wine and Food Festival

'We have sent wine to every continent on earth, even to Antarctica; and we offer more than 1,600 labels of South African wines in our large store.'

Cathy and Paul du Toit, Wine Village, specialist wine shop

Voted one of South Africa's top 10 wine festivals, this annual event showcases the premier wine producers of the Cape South Coast and features a large food marquee that will delight all epicureans. The spirit of the festival is evident in its organisers' passion to promote excellent South African wines, the best craft beers and top-of-the-crop local food.

Hosted by the Wine Village, the festival is a prestigious and increasingly popular event on the wine industry calendar. Each August, the viticulture of the region, represented by the many diverse wines, wineries and winemakers, from Hermanus and Walker Bay to Elgin and Elim, is celebrated. The region has grown from six wine producers in 1998 to the current count of more than 65 premium wine and craft beer producers. As the festival approaches 21 years of existence, this prize-winning event with its convivial atmosphere offers a vino experience not to be missed.

The Hermanus Wine and Food Festival, organised by Paul du Toit (opposite) and his wife, Cathy, offers a fabulous feast of artisanal breads, cheeses, quality olive oil, seafood delights and fruits of the vine – a true celebration of local cellar and culinary creations.

HERMANUS 105

Kalfiefees

The Kalfiefees, synonymous with whales and winter and focusing on Afrikaans culture, takes place annually during August in Onrus.

The Kalfiefees showcases an extravaganza of top performing artists. Each year, the festival organisers line up a premier programme of theatre and drama, featuring a variety of genres ranging from comedy and music to cabaret and literature.

In 2015 the Kalfiefees presented a celebration of the iconic South African poet, Ingrid Jonker, who tragically died in 1965 at the age of 32. The event was created in memory of her death 50 years ago. Ingrid Jonker was one of the Sestigers, a literary group also known as the *Beweging van Sestig* ('the movement of sixty'). Some members of this movement, such as Jan Rabie and Uys Krige, lived in Hermanus.

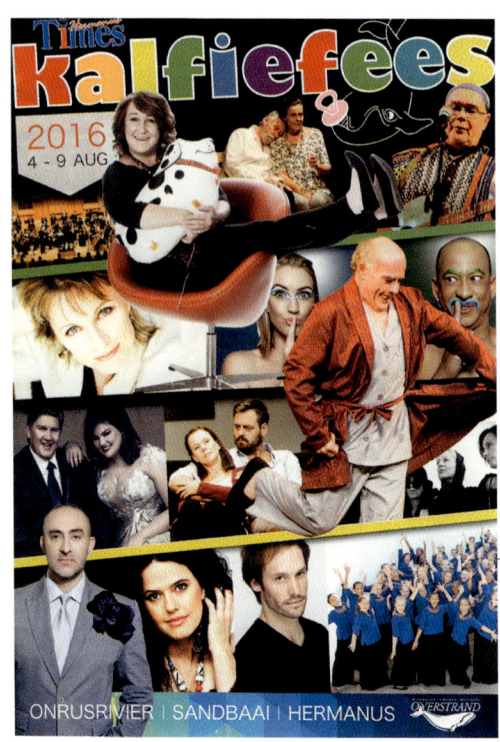

THE SESTIGERS

During the early 1960s a new literary movement, known as the Sestigers ('generation of the Sixties'), embraced secularization, modernity, racial tolerance and sexual freedom, and used modern literary techniques and subject matter to explore these themes ... This literature helped to change the political imagination of the Afrikaans reading public in subtle yet profound ways.

They offered a new conceptualization of the Afrikaners and their history that differed starkly from the image the political leaders and cultural leadership tried to project of the Afrikaners as a people determined to crush all threats to their survival.

Hermann Giliomee, historian and author of *The Afrikaners: Biography of a People*, 2003

Internationally acclaimed chanteuse, actress and playwright Daniele Pascal (far left) is a regular performer at the Kalfiefees, a festival of theatre and music held at several venues in Onrus, Sandbaai and Hermanus every August.

The Hermanus Whale Festival

The Hermanus Whale Festival stars Walker Bay's marine celebrities in a series of spectacular performances: from breaching to spyhopping, sailing, blowing and grunting to a grand finale of playing with kelp. In addition to whale watching from the shore, the festival also offers an Eco Marine Village, great food, quality crafters, sports events, entertainment for the young, a classic car show, music performances, and loads of fun in the sun – all this while enjoying the natural environment in the whale capital of the world!

This annual celebration of the whales in the bay, which usually takes place in spring, at the end of September, is the only enviro-arts event in South Africa.

After 25 festivals, the stars of the show are, as always (of course), the whales.

Highlights of the Hermanus Whale Festival include the Whales and Wheels Classic Car Show (bottom left), acrobatic street performers (bottom right), a street parade and live music performances.

HERMANUS 107

HERMANUS ON THE MAP

'"Hermanus is unique!"
I have heard this acclamation not once but a dozen times. Yet when you press people to explain they have difficulty, for its charm is elusive; it means many things to many people.'

Hermanus – A Guide to the Riviera of the South, Jose Burman, 1989

Hermanus, the Overberg town of which Burman writes in his book, had its humble origins in the discovery of a spring and a favourable place to graze a flock of sheep. Soon after, it was to become an angler's Shangri-La. Little did the fisherfolk know back then that the nucleus of their world, the Old Harbour, would in time become one of the villlage's most recognisable landmarks, and an official heritage site. But there are several other attributes that have put Hermanus on the map: whether natural or constructed, they all add to the uniqueness of this popular town.

When Burman wrote his book almost 30 years ago, he noted the town's effort to preserve elements of its heritage: 'At the only main-road robot, the heart of the commercial centre is occupied, not by a hypermarket or other high-pressure business establishment, but by another anomaly – a museum project, a fishing-village complex with a village green.'

Looking at the layout of the town, you will notice the many unique features that have made Hermanus such a distinctive place. It has two harbours, one old, the other new; an international space agency; a modern shopping mall located a stone's throw from a cave that has yielded evidence of human habitation some 70,000 years ago; a scenic golf course rated as one of the finest in the country; and a railway station that has never had a train pass through it.

A fishing boat moored at the New Harbour quayside. The New Harbour, which became operational in 1951, offered better protection against storms and improved mooring facilities.

HERMANUS 109

Lemm's Corner

'Skip the chains and the over-hyped spots with sea views. Fisherman's Cottage situated on Lemm's Corner serves superb seafood in a cosy atmosphere. Great for lunch or a fairly light enhanced evening dinner. Best calamari I've ever tasted, but plenty good on the menu aside from that.'

Customer's comment on TripAdvisor

The original village of Hermanus consisted of an enclave of fishermen's cottages, some of which have today been restored as heritage sites. At Lemm's Corner, situated in the heart of Hermanus, a ring wall encloses the lawned village green with its copse of shady stinkwood trees. Here, a number of the renovated fishermen's cottages have been converted into speciality shops, including the well-known Fisherman's Cottage restaurant.

The nostalgic atmosphere of Lemm's Corner, evocative of a quaint fishing village, is showcased at De Wet's Huis Photographic Museum, where you can take a step back into the past and immerse yourself in an exhibition of historical photographs and memorabilia. The building, previously a schoolhouse standing at the Dutch Reformed Church in Westcliff, was dismantled brick by brick and reconstructed on the Fishermen's Village site in 1987. Nearby is the Whale Museum, displaying the skeleton of one of the world's largest mammals. The museum holds daily audiovisual presentations about whales and dolphins.

The name of this historic corner derives from Mr Bernard Lemonsky, who in the 1960s rented a building on the property which he ran as Lemm's Stores. He and his family lived above the shop, which was also to become home to the first bioscope in Hermanus. The Victorian-style building has sadly since been demolished. In June 1983 Lemm's Corner was purchased by the Old Harbour Museum.

Another preserved area, close to Hermanus Pieters's freshwater spring, is Swallow Park. This was once a piece of wasteland, but in the early 1900s it became the dream of a local schoolteacher, Magdalena Neethling, to turn it into a lovely garden park. This strong-willed teacher was nicknamed Swallow because of her petite size and darting movements. Once given the go-ahead from the authorities for a park, she gardened tirelessly so as to give back something to the village she loved. During her lifetime, the park was laid out with rockeries and two fountains. Today, a group of venerable pines and palm trees keeps vigil over this special heritage spot.

LEARNING FROM HISTORY

There are many lessons to be learned from history. My analysis of the economic history of Hermanus and other towns in the Overstrand illustrates one big lesson: do not overdevelop your town and reduce or destroy the attractions for which many people come to the town. Conserve your history wherever you can. The economic future of Hermanus lies in environmental and adventure tourism. It is damaging our own future to permit conservation areas to be encroached upon by development or to encourage investment in shopping malls that no tourist wants to enter, rather than smaller retail outlets that tourists want to use.

Dr Robin Lee, What is Hermanus's heritage?, *The Village News*, September 2016

The historic Fishermen's Village is the site of museums, restaurants, shops and a market.

HERMANUS 111

HERMANUS

The Old Harbour

'The fishermen know that the sea is dangerous and the storm terrible, but they have never found these dangers sufficient reason for remaining on shore.'

Vincent van Gogh

In the early days of Hermanus, it was from the Old Harbour, then known as Visbaai ('fish bay'), that wives waved to their husbands as they went to sea, and then waited and watched for their safe return. In those early, pioneering days, fishermen set out in rowing boats, pitting their strength against the remorseless ocean. Down at the rocky cove, with its buzz of activity, fish hauls were cleaned, gutted, salted in brine and packed for transport.

The return of the fishing boats to the inlet was the event of the day – and continued to be so for more than a century. Often, the boats had to ride the waves outside the harbour in heavy seas, waiting for a break between swells before the fishermen could row in their small vessels. The last boats used the harbour in 1958, and in 1970 the Old Harbour was declared a heritage site.

Market day, with its fabulous tales of fish hauls, monster sharks and mariners' lives lost at sea, is now part of a bygone era. The renovated Old Harbour, with its indoor museum housed in old fishermen's huts on the slopes, its fishing boats and its cement gutting tables, stands as a tribute to a place that once thrummed with the activities and lives of the early seamen and their families.

The Old Harbour, with its fishermen's huts, boats and cement fish-gutting tables, was proclaimed a heritage site in 1970.

Close to the Old Harbour is Bientang's Cave, named after a Khoikhoi woman who reputedly lived in the cave.

The days of casual fishing are gone. Due to severe marine depletion and the negative human impact on the coast, it is now necessary to obtain a permit for angling. A permit is also required to dive for crayfish (rock lobster) and perlemoen (abalone).

A well-known historic landmark not far from the Old Harbour is the Burgundy Restaurant. Originally called the Cypress Tree Tea Garden, it was opened in 1928 by an Englishwoman, Ethel Rubery. It attained legendary status by offering a genteel Victorian ambience in an idyllic seafront setting. Later the Hemel-en-Aarde wine pioneer, Timothy Hamilton Russell, purchased the restaurant and introduced a continental style to the establishment by renaming it the Burgundy, in celebration of the local Pinot Noirs and Chardonnays. Also near the Old Harbour is Bientang's Cave, accessible down a flight of steps from the Cliff Path. This internationally famous restaurant is set in an ancient cave, where you dine with the waves and the whales at your elbow.

The legend of Bientang originates from the last known Khoikhoi Strandloper, who lived in the cave at the turn of the nineteenth century. A pioneering free spirit, Bientang drew water from a mountain stream, which to this day still runs beneath the staircase at the cave's entrance. She lived on fruit and vegetables from her garden and the fresh fish she caught from the rocks. Bientang was believed to have had supernatural powers and a spiritual sensitivity towards nature and the whales. She was reputed to guard her humble abode with a zealous passion, and no one dared trespass in her domain. It was also claimed that a family of spotted genet cats were her constant companions; folklore has it that they still inhabit the surrounding cliffs.

Further along the cliffs, Gearing's Point is one of the most popular whale-watching sites in the town, where wraparound vistas of the Old Harbour and Walker Bay can be enjoyed from the comfort

The brightly illustrated display boards at Gearing's Point provide an informative overview of Walker Bay's marine and bird life.

Hermanus histories

Roger Bushell, architect of The Great Escape, was born in South Africa. He spent many of his boyhood holidays at his parents' seaside cottage in Hermanus. As a squadron leader and fighter pilot in the Royal Air Force, he was shot down in 1940 and sent to a POW camp. After his third escape attempt and recapture in 1944, he and the other escapees were executed under a specific order given by Hitler. Roger Bushell was buried in Poland, but his name also appears on the war memorial in Hermanus, where his parents spent their last years and where they were buried.

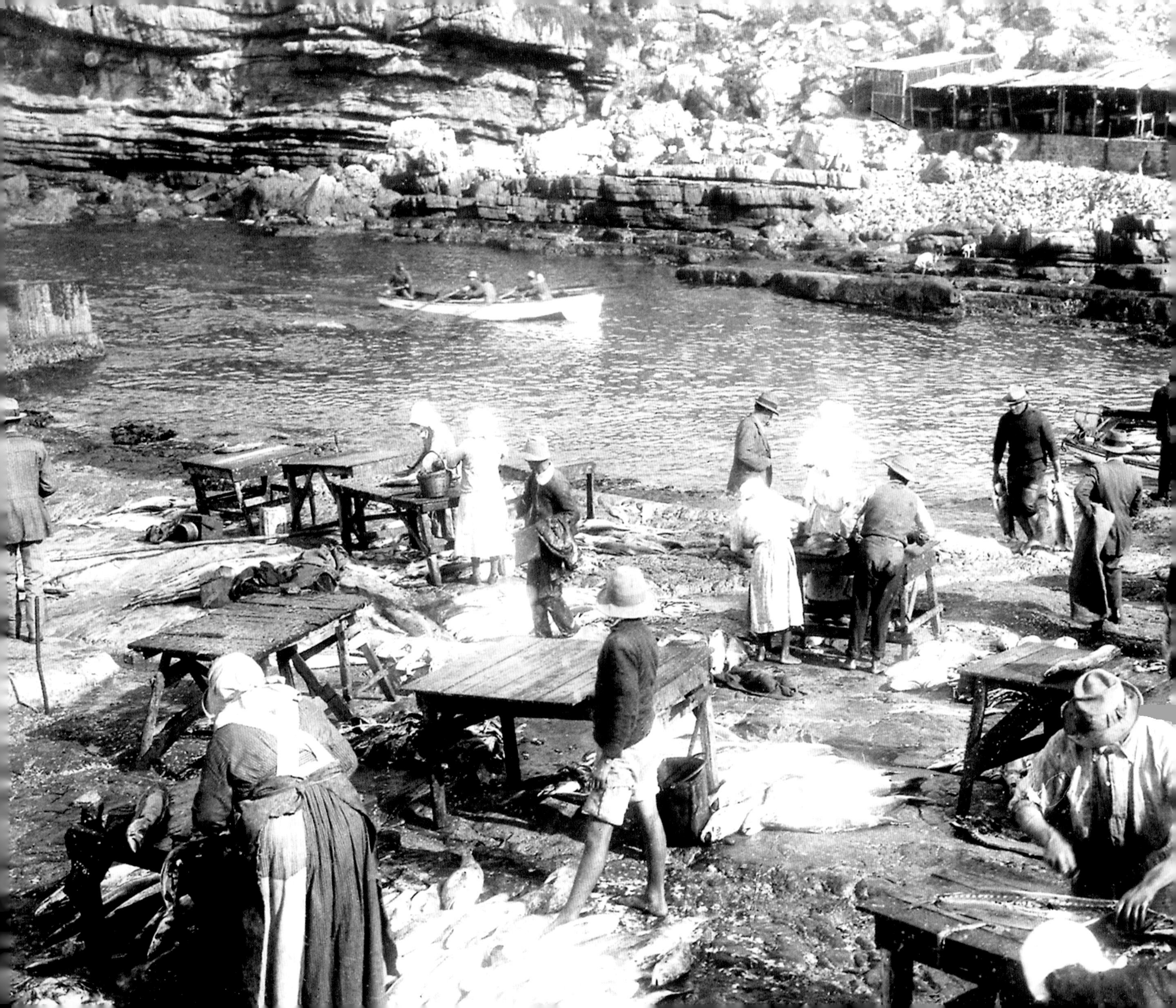

Hermanus histories

In the 1950s, a tidal wave swept across the bay, awful, majestic, measuring 20 metres in height, washing over Gearing's Point, sweeping up the grass bank, across the road and into the sanatorium. The Coloured people living in caves near the harbour took flight. Its force wreaked havoc as far as the Klein River Lagoon, flooding farmlands on its shores. When the water was sucked back into the sea, the image of death was strewn across the land with dead fish, perlemoen, red bait, and corals wreathed in ragged seaweed.

Arderne Tredgold, Village of the Sea – The Story of Hermanus, 1965

of your car in all types of weather. It is a regular destination for visiting tourist coaches, and also a favoured community club for seagulls and dassies.

Harbour House, just across the way from Gearing's Point, was once the site of the rustic home of a local fisherman, Bill Selkirk, who became an overnight sensation when he caught his famous shark. Back then, Gearing's Point was an idyllic rendezvous for the fisherfolk; the aroma of a seafood braai might waft on the ocean breeze, and locals came together to celebrate special events and New Year, dancing beneath the stars to the music of a concertina and guitar. Even though the modern tempo has altered the rhythm of the town, the heart of Hermanus remains in tune with the memory of those bygone days.

Harbour House is one of the most distinctive landmarks in Hermanus, and commands an impressive outlook across the rocky promontory at Gearing's Point, witnessing the ocean's changing moods and the passing of time. This historical home has been converted into a luxurious five-star hotel with a state-of-the-art swimming pool, bordered by the sea on one side and Harbour Road on the other. Harbour Road is probably the shortest retail street in Hermanus, with its mélange of art galleries, restaurants and speciality shops.

In the vicinity, above the Old Harbour, a mounted telescope enables viewing of whales in the deeper waters of the bay.

In both World Wars, it is recorded that Hermanus sent a larger number of volunteers to the front than any other village in South Africa. A memorial above the Old Harbour pays tribute to the fallen; it consists of a cenotaph flanked by two naval cannon that face the town, in a token of peace to approaching ships.

For decades, small fishing boats would bring their catch ashore at the Old Harbour, where it would be gutted and sold on the spot, or salted and packaged for sale further afield.

HERMANUS

The New Harbour

'The oceans are Earth's most dynamic environment. They contain about 135 billion km³ of water, and this huge mass is constantly on the move. The surface waters rock back and forth as waves pass over, from gentle ripples to powerful swells whipped up by storms. Twice a day, in response to the gravitational forces of the Sun and Moon, the tides rise and fall, their continual motion gradually eroding and shaping the land.'

Daniel Gilpin, *The Mighty Oceans*, 2006

As the fishing industry took off in Hermanus there was a need to build a harbour with a large breakwater for protection against storms, and where trawlers could be moored.

The New Harbour at Still Bay was conceived in the late 1920s, but the project stalled due to a lack of funding during the Great Depression. A start was made in 1939, but it again went on hold with the advent of World War II. Full construction recommenced in 1946 and the harbour was completed in 1951. Today, this small harbour, with its headland at the end of Westcliff, is part of a commercial network of abalone, crayfish and fish-canning factories. Perlemoen is cultivated at vast aquaculture farms in the surrounds of the New Harbour. These land-based farms house the slow-growing gastropods in tanks and baskets. Seawater is pumped through the containers day and night to sustain them.

Should you wish to know more about the spawning, stages of development, and harvest of these grey molluscs, you could consider a conducted farm tour at Abagold, one of the oldest and largest abalone farms in South Africa.

In winter, during the 'snoek run', the New Harbour is a hive of activity as fishing boats unload large catches of snoek. The fish are cleaned and gutted before being sold to eager buyers.

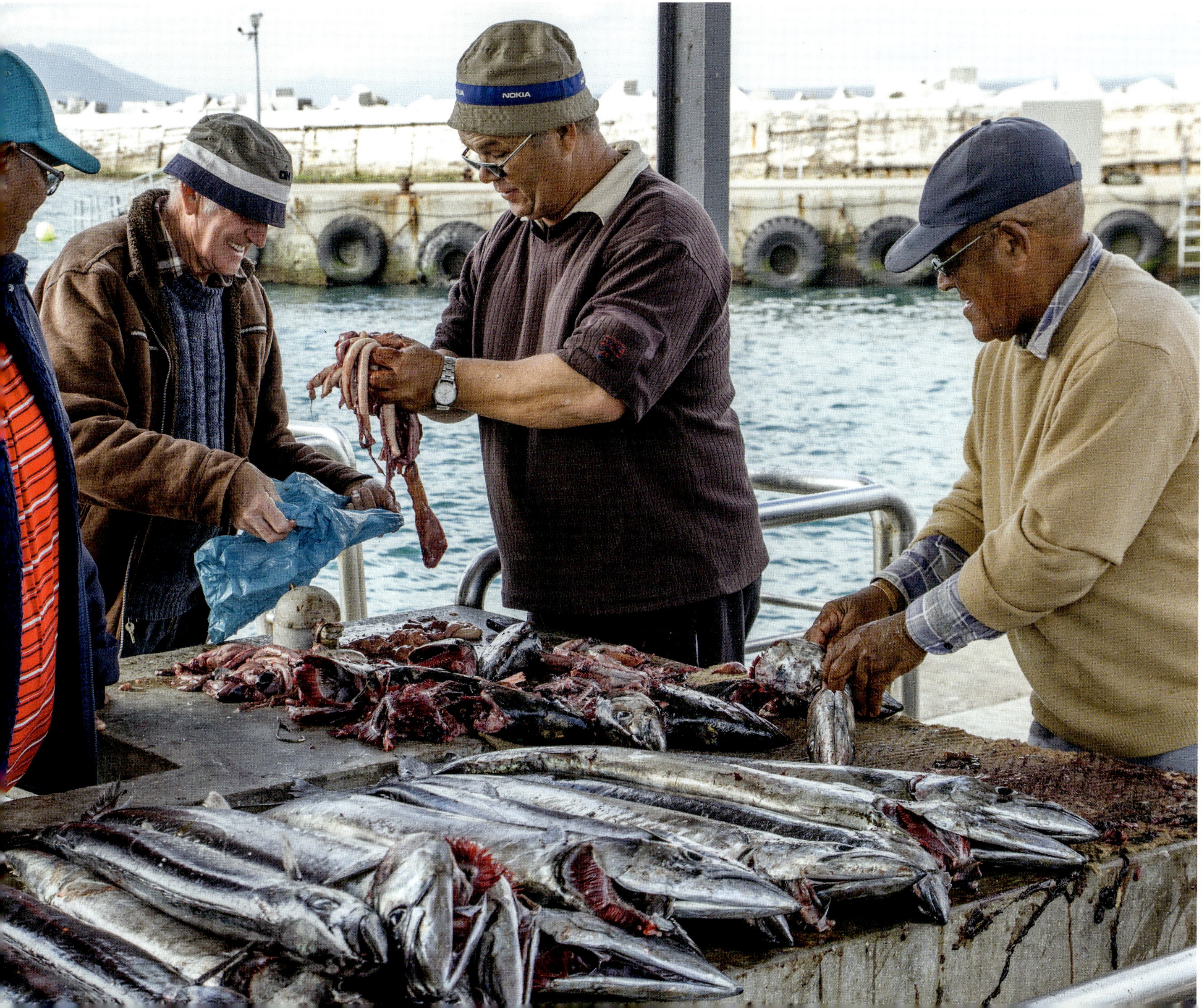
NOKIA

A drive to the New Harbour takes you along a boulevard of guesthouses, boutique hotels and residential homes, all with framed sea views overlooking the Cliff Path. As you pass the National Sea Rescue Institute's headquarters, turn down towards the quay. Brightly painted trawlers moored along the wharf side, with names like *Lorelei*, *Santa Isabella*, *Arizon II* and *Melissa Kelly*, sway in the wind while the gulls wheel above. Those who have a passion for the ocean will sense the adventure of a harbour and its maritime romance … the stories seamen bring back with them about nautical mysteries, savage predators, pirates and the lives lost in those watery depths. Each boat berthed here has its own tale to tell.

Today they are unloading pilchards. Fishermen in their yellow oilskins move about on deck and throw offal to the shrieking gulls. Down at the dock, the Quayside Cabin, specialising in food harvested from the ocean, invites you to experience the conviviality of harbour life. *Bon appétit* as you watch the waves plunging over the *dolosse* (concrete blocks that form a breakwater) and the boats chugging in to unload their catch at the quayside.

The wharf is also a good place to watch whales and seals doing aquabatics. Bring your own rod and take up the challenge of baiting a big fish, or board a boat and chill out on a whale-watching cruise. The charters leave daily during whale season. Sundowner and eco-marine cruises are also available.

While large commercial fishing companies have long since moved their fleets to bigger harbours, the New Harbour is still used by some trawlers and line fishermen.

The renowned Harbour Rock restaurant is set above the port, on a rocky outcrop at the cliff's edge. Along with a delicious selection of seafood, sushi and other traditional delights, you will be treated to wraparound views of Westcliff – taking in the Windsor Hotel – as well as Rotary Way, Babylonstoren and beyond, all the way to Gansbaai.

The South African word for abalone, 'perlemoen', is derived from the Dutch term *paarlemoer* (mother of pearl), which is what is found on the inside of the protective shell of the animal.

The San and the Khoikhoi first fished for perlemoen 125,000 years ago, when resources were plentiful. The modern perlemoen industry was pioneered in 1952 by one man paying children sixpence for each large 'sea snail' picked off the rocks. Over the years, the trade escalated into a massive export market.

At one time, professional divers could bring in between 2,000 and 6,000 perlemoen a day at the height of the open season and in perfect conditions. A screwdriver was the only tool needed to prise them from the rocks. Unfortunately, with over-harvesting, abalone has become scarce, and it is illegal to take them from the ocean without a permit. It takes eight to nine years for this sea delicacy to grow to the minimum legal size for harvesting.

Today the industry is strictly controlled, with quota allocations and limits on divers and equipment, with the result that many legitimate fishermen and divers have been forced out of their occupation. Rampant poaching, driven by illegal syndicates and fuelled by markets in the Far East, results in the indiscriminate removal of perlemoen from the seabed and threatens the survival of the species.

MAKING CHANGES

There are future plans in the pipeline for the New Harbour. Government funding may change several small harbours, no longer used for fishing, into recreational and tourism sites. This has been done with great success in several countries. In Hermanus the existing Lusitania building will be converted into a salmon farm and upgrading will include more moorings for boats.

The Village News, October 2016

A fisherman tends to a boat in the New Harbour.

The South African National Space Agency

It is believed that the compass was invented in China, but it was the European explorers who first made practical use of it. They relied on the compass needle pointing north, and thus devised a system of navigation. During the great era of exploration, between 1600 and 1700, visiting seamen from Europe were responsible for early magnetic observations in South Africa. Cornelis Houtman, commander of a Dutch fleet on its way to India, made the earliest recorded observation of magnetic declination on land at Mossel Bay in 1595, obtaining a value of 0°. The Portuguese word *agulhas* (which means 'needles') was given to the southernmost tip of Africa in the early 1600s when compass needles there were found to point directly towards true north.

The deviation of the earth's magnetic field directly affects navigation by compass, and this must be taken into account by navigators. Today, the needle points 24 degrees west of true north in Hermanus.

The first systematic magnetic observations in South Africa resulted from the establishment, in 1841, of a worldwide network of observation stations. One of these stations was built in the grounds of the Royal Observatory at the Cape of Good Hope; the Royal Artillery detachment was responsible for all measurements. After this magnetic observatory was destroyed by fire in 1852, 80 years were to pass before a new magnetic observatory worthy of the name was established in South Africa.

The Polar Year 1932–1933 prompted the establishment of a magnetic observatory at the University of Cape Town in 1932, under the leadership of Professor Alexander Ogg. International organisations provided grants for buildings and loaned the observatory instruments for standard observations. The subsequent electrification of the suburban railway network, however, disturbed the instruments, to the extent that accurate observations became almost impossible.

A new site was identified in Hermanus, because it was sufficiently remote from electric railway disturbances and had been proven by a magnetic survey to be 'magnetically clean'. This is because the rock structure in Hermanus consists mainly of Cape sandstone, with no traceable magnetism. The Hermanus Magnetic Observatory officially commenced operation on 1 January 1941.

Now known as the South African National Space Agency (SANSA) Space Science facility, its purpose, like other magnetic observatories worldwide, is to record the variations in the earth's magnetic field, to analyse these phenomena, and to distribute magnetic information internationally to other researchers and geophysicists. It exploits ground observations as well as data from low-earth-orbit satellites to investigate the peculiar behaviour of the magnetic field over southern Africa. Mathematical models derived from ground survey measurements are extensively used in navigation technologies.

Since the first observatory was founded in Cape Town in 1841, geomagnetism research has grown in stature. One of the major contributions to geomagnetism research in southern Africa was the institution of a long-term magnetic secular variation programme in 1938–1939. The programme initially comprised 44 permanent field stations covering more or less uniformly the whole of South Africa, Namibia and Botswana; it has since been expanded to 75 stations and its coverage now includes Zimbabwe.

The SANSA Space Science directorate in Hermanus monitors the earth's electromagnetic field and space weather conditions close to earth. Hermanus is well suited to this type of investigation, as the environment here is relatively free from magnetic interference.

Hoy's Koppie

'Nature does not hurry, yet everything is accomplished.'

Lao Tzu

William Hoy was a regular guest at the Marine Hotel from 1910 until his death in 1930. This dynamic self-educated Scotsman was appointed the first general manager of the South African Railways at the age of 40. He was knighted six years later.

A keen fisherman, reputedly the fastest shorthand scribe in South Africa and owner of the first typewriter in the country, he was all for protecting the exclusivity of his angling paradise with its bracing champagne air. During peak seasons he had seen beaches such as Kalk Bay in the Cape bursting at the seams with holiday crowds each time the train pulled into the station. For that reason, he opposed the planned railway line extending from Bot River to Hermanus.

Hoy's policy succeeded. To this day, neither the station building in Hermanus nor the railway bridge over the Bot River has ever seen a train!

At his request, Sir William Hoy was buried on top of the koppie he so loved to climb. Lady Gertrude Hoy passed away in England, but her body was brought back to Hermanus to be buried alongside that of her husband.

A resident and his dogs enjoy the view from Hoy's Koppie, where Sir William Hoy and his wife, Lady Gertrude, lie buried.

The hill named after Sir William Hoy is at Eastcliff and is accessible on foot from town. A path leads up to the summit, where you can view the historic stone crypts. From here, the vista sweeps over the rooftops of the town, with its backdrop of mountains and Walker Bay. In today's suburban sprawl, this green lung is a protected area, inhabited by dassies and tortoises and surrounded by aloes and fynbos, comprising at least 300 species.

The carving of a Bushman's head was discovered in a large cave on the southern side of Hoy's Koppie. Archaeological evidence shows that the Khoisan once lived in this rocky shelter, now known as Klipkop ('rock-head') Cave, long before Hermanus Pieters arrived with his flock of sheep.

Hermanus histories

When William Hoy retired, the Rhodesian government offered him a post in charge of the railways, which he accepted. He continued to spend his holidays in Hermanus, where over the years he enjoyed 18 summer vacations at the Marine Hotel. His last trip to the village he loved was in 1930.

The Hermanus Golf Club

'Between Walker Bay and the Klein River Mountains lies one of the most treasured pieces of land, the Hermanus golf course. It is here, in this unique location, that we have created over the past 100 years not just a golf club, but a way of life for so many of us.'

Hannes Kleynhans, President of the Hermanus Golf Club,
Hermanus Golf Club Centenary Album 1907–2007, 2007

The Klein River Mountains form a dramatic backdrop to the Hermanus golf course.

Golf had humble beginnings in Hermanus. The original municipal golf course in Westcliff, built in 1907, was unsuccessful. Later, a nine-hole course was laid out on the commonage ground at Poole's Bay. John Luyt, owner of the Marine Hotel, was the prime mover in having the golf course relocated to a more favourable position for hotel guests. He put together a plan for the Governor-General of the Union of South Africa, HRH Prince Arthur of Connaught, to open the golf club in an official ceremony when he travelled from the United Kingdom to the Cape for the 1923 parliamentary session. Once he had declared the course open, Prince Arthur played the first ball. In celebration of the event, a dance was held that evening with pomp and splendour in the dining room of the Marine Hotel.

In 1936 the golf course was redesigned with 18 holes.

A year before its centenary, the Hermanus Golf Club again underwent a major overhaul with the introduction of a further nine holes. Superb new greens and bunkering have been introduced, and the course has been considerably lengthened. The upgrade and redesign have been combined with the introduction of new pockets of real estate, which have been cleverly interspersed among the fairways without impacting on the original charm of the golfing experience. The new, classically designed holes have added much to the visual appeal and challenge of the course, without losing any sense of its former tradition.

This 27-hole masterpiece is popular among local residents and visitors, especially during the Christmas and Easter holidays. In recent years, international visitors have also discovered the course. The Hermanus Golf Club showcases a prestigious annual event, the Walker Bay Classic – a golfing extravaganza that has 'aced' each of the 30 years of its existence.

The golf course, flanked by mountains, has introduced three springbok to its scenic tree-lined landscape. These beautiful buck enhance the appeal of the fairways and can often be seen grazing on the greens. Baboons are also regular visitors, and 'birdies' of the feathered kind include francolins, guineafowl and Egyptian geese – making this a truly African golfing safari.

Hermanus histories

The Prince and Princess were accommodated on their visit to Hermanus in Schoongezicht, the home belonging to John Luyt, owner of the Marine Hotel. Sir William Hoy, general manager of South African Railways and Harbours, loaned the chef and two waiters from the White Train to cater for the royal couple. Hermanus was agog when the Princess officiated at a ball held at the Marine. At the golf course ceremony next day, an escort of mounted police, in pith helmets with rifles raised in salute, lent a regal and military air to the occasion. Their paraded ranks of finely groomed grey mounts possibly hid from view the cows grazing on Poole's Bay common as they pushed at the fences that kept them off the lush new greens.

Rex Gibson and Harvey Tyson, *Hermanus Golf Club Centenary Album 1907–2007*, 2007

Hermanus golfers having fun on the greens.

128   HERMANUS

THE NATURAL BEAUTY OF HERMANUS

'The footpath that old Hermanus Pieters trod with his sheep from the valley to reach the sea crosses Rotary Way and I turned to look at the scene that unfolded before him as he reached the mountain's crest. It was even more beautiful than that behind me. The satin blue sea was the wide heart of it, washing into the curve of the bay from the far south, sending its pulses in long smooth curves to break in foam on the beach ...'

Arderne Tredgold, *Village of the Sea – The Story of Hermanus*, 1965

From the silence of the mountains at Rotary Way to the rhythm of the ocean waves below, the unique beauty of Hermanus is inescapable and compelling. Like all coastlines, the one that cradles this seaside village has its own moods and qualities, which can only be experienced by spending time here.

The Hermanus coastline is further enhanced by its many beautiful beaches – from the glorious stretch of golden sand at Grotto Beach, ideal for long meditative walks, to the expansive seashore of Onrus Beach, a firm family favourite and a popular choice with surfers. Here, where land and sea meet, you are invited to relax beneath an umbrella and enjoy the warmth of the sun and the sound of the ocean.

Spanning two kilometres from Voëlklip to the mouth of the Klein River Lagoon, Grotto Beach is one of the most popular destinations along the Hermanus coastline. To the north-east of the lagoon lies the Walker Bay Nature Reserve and further along are the cliffs of De Kelders. A stroll along this vast expanse can calm the mind and soothe the soul.

Grotto Beach offers a safe and clean environment to simply relax, or cool down in the crystal-clear waters of the Atlantic. Parking is provided next to the beach.

The beaches

'The beach is not a place to work; to read, write or to think.'

Anne Morrow Lindbergh

The white sands that start at Grotto Beach extend for 22 kilometres along the bay, past the Klein River Lagoon and Die Plaat to the rocky cliffs of De Kelders further down the coast. This Blue Flag beach invites you to take long strolls along its shoreline or to recharge your batteries with vigorous jogging. Outside the area demarcated by flying flags, the beach is also dog-friendly.

The Blue Flag Award is a symbol of excellence, conceived in France in 1985, that sets stringent standards in respect of beach management, environmental ethics and amenities offered. South Africa is the first country outside Europe to have introduced this initiative.

A walk along Grotto Beach at different times of the day, observing the changing moods of this spectacular seascape, can be a meditative experience as you tune in to the mantra of the surf and fill your lungs with the bracing ozone-rich air. Watch the *sterretjies* (terns) wheeling in a white symphony above, then turning in perfect unison before disappearing from sight.

Grotto Beach was originally named Riviera Beach, but its name was changed when the grottos in the cliffs behind the beach were opened. A short distance from the sea, there is an ancient cave

SAFETY, QUALITY AND ACCESS FOR ALL

The Blue Flag programme offers many benefits: improved tourism facilities, enhanced management of coastal ecosystems, increased awareness of the coast, and providing beachgoers and visitors with the assurance of world-class beaches with safe, clean and well-managed facilities. Also included as part of the programme is a Blue Flag accreditation system to acknowledge sustainable boating operators in the tourism industry. South Africa is at the forefront of this project and is one of only three Blue Flag member countries to have received accreditation for sustainable boating operators in the 2016/2017 season. The accredited operators, and their boats, are Dyer Island Cruises (*Whale Whisperer* and *Dream Catcher*) and Marine Dynamics (*The Slashfin*).

The Village News, October 2016

carved out of rock beneath a grove of milkwood trees. Over time, an ecology of lichen, moss-covered stone and a variety of ferns and other plant life has been created by the constant dripping of water from the overhanging crags.

The surrounding forest of milkwood trees known as Piet-se-Bos offers a glade of shade and shelter from the wind. Milkwoods have been growing in this area for centuries. Because of the decrease in their numbers through development, fire and invasive alien vegetation, they are now a protected species.

Milkwoods (*Sideroxylon inerme*) can grow to a height of about ten metres, with their sheltering canopies providing homes to birds and boomslangs. The birds and baboons feed on the purplish-black berries, and the flowers attract insects with their pungent smell. The name of the tree is taken from the milky latex present in the bark and fruit. African folklore claims that an infusion of the bark will dispel nightmares.

The beaches along the beautiful coastline of Hermanus are many and varied. Below the rambling cliffs you will find a network of sandy coves with reefs of rock, each having its own natural intertidal characteristics.

Voëlklip Beach, stretching down from terraced lawns, is one of the most popular spots, attracting flocks of sun-worshippers, surfers and bathers in summer.

Lying alongside Voëlklip Beach is Kammabaai, also known as Nanny's Beach. This name apparently originated in earlier times when Caledon farmers visited the town for family holidays. The

Hermanus is known for its variety of beaches, from the pristine Grotto Beach (above) to the immensely popular Voëlklip Beach (below).

'non-white' nannies supervising the children were allowed to swim on one side of a huge rock jutting out to sea, while the 'Europeans' swam on the other side. This beach is also sometimes known as Lover's Cove.

Another perennial favourite on the list is Langbaai, with its long tracts of rocky coves. Some beaches are ideal for surfing; others for sheltered sunbathing; and those with tidal pools are safe for swimming. The beach at Langbaai is great for taking a dip in the waves, but always pay attention to the changing tides, and take heed of the old fisherman's warning: 'Never turn your back to the sea.' Langbaai is the last stretch of beach before the cliffs ascend, taking walkers along the Cliff Path to view scenic panoramas across the bay as far as the New Harbour.

The suburbs of Sandbaai, Onrus and Vermont, along the coastline to the west, have beautiful beaches, rocky reefs and tidal pools.

One of the natural seawater inlets, improved by dynamiting the rocks, is Fick's Pool, situated close to Hermanus Pieters's spring at Westcliff. In days gone by Fick's Pool even boasted a row of bathing boxes. In its heyday, it was a trendy place to be. Today the most popular tidal pool, known as Bientang se Baaigat ('Bientang's swimming hole'), lies below the Cliff Path and The Marine hotel. Here safe bathing can be enjoyed in both outgoing and incoming tides. The small pebbly shoreline is strewn with rocks leading up to a concrete deck that houses an ablution block and outdoor shower. Over the years, groups of brave bathers have made it a ritual to gather here for energising early-morning dips, undaunted by the weather or the icy water.

The boulders and slabs of flat crags below the cliffs also offer a close-up view of whales – at times you can even hear their resonant blowing as they languidly swim past beds of brown kelp shimmering in the water.

Organised walking beach safaris provide guided tours along the seashore, connecting you with the different moods of the ocean. Unique trails combine evening sundowners, meals and accommodation close enough to be lulled to sleep by the symphony of the surf.

Horseback riding is another way to appreciate the beach and its beautiful surrounds. Horse trails evoke a sense of freedom and adventure; there are rides to Grotto Beach and along Die Plaat, with its vast stretch of sand, all the way to De Kelders.

The sea and sand are ideal playgrounds for a variety of activities, from surfing and touch rugby to frolicking in the waves.

The Cliff Path

*'Sit and do nothing —
the grass will grow by itself.'*

Zen saying

A memorable feature to experience on a visit to Hermanus is its famous Cliff Path. From any point, you can take in an impressive aspect of this spectacular showpiece, with its natural rock formation skirting the ocean. Spanning 12 kilometres, the path winds its way along the coastline from the New Harbour in the west, traversing the town, to the estuary at the mouth of the Klein River in the east.

If you stand on the Cliff Path's boardwalk opposite Swallow Park, near where Hermanus Pieters set up camp, you may experience the same sensations as he did, as you watch the streams cascading down the mossy rock face before spilling into the shady deep pool cove below, and hear the reverberating echo of the waves in the background.

The Cliff Path, with its fragile ecosystem and fynbos terrain, was incorporated into the Fernkloof Nature Reserve in 2000. Part of the path between Gearing's Point and the Hermanuspietersfontein spring is known as Champagne Mile. Gearing's Point, always a popular viewing site for whales, has recently been embellished with an open-air gallery featuring modern sculptures. This initiative by Hermanus FynArts brings an added dimension to the path experience.

Spanning 12 kilometres from the New Harbour through the town to the Klein River Lagoon in the east, the Cliff Path hugs the coastline, wending its way through coastal fynbos, past jagged rocks and along pristine beaches.

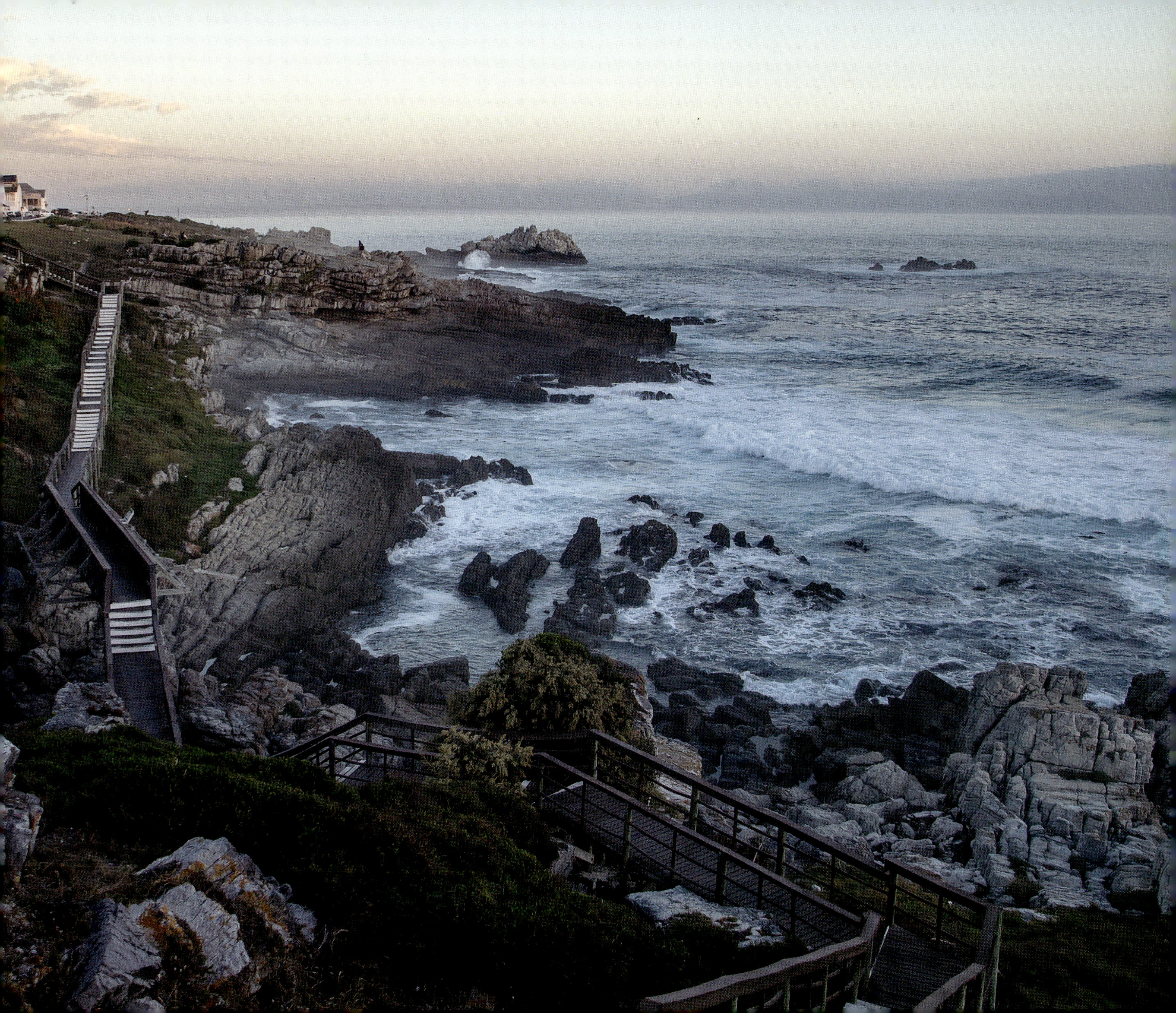

The path is dotted with benches from where one can take in the tranquil views across the bay.

The view from Tamatiebank towards Preekstoel, looking east. Both these landmarks, between the New Harbour and Fick's Pool, are well-known fishing spots.

Culture and education go hand in hand; it is also here that the Hermanus Biodiversity Walk begins. Follow the trail to find out more about the multiple components that constitute the natural biodiversity of this beautiful stretch of the Walker Bay coastline. Illustrated storyboards positioned along the path provide you with information about topics ranging from urbanisation and its impact on nature to invasive plants and the threat of fire. It is sobering to read that the Western Cape has the highest extinction rate of plant species in the world.

As you pause to read the information boards, you will soon discover that you are stepping into a remarkable natural environment inhabited by many different bird, frog and plant species. As one of the storyboards states: 'The mammals and reptiles that occur along the Walker Bay coastline are all integral to its biodiversity.' Common species to watch for are rock dassies, Cape clawless otters, Cape dwarf chameleons, porcupines, striped mice, large grey mongooses, Cape flat lizards and mole snakes. It is interesting to note that names of local animals and plants often have Khoikhoi origins. Examples are *gogga* (insect); *buchu* and *dagga* (plants); and *quagga* and *kudu* (animals).

An intriguing snippet on one of the information nodes tells us that the ladybird (ladybeetle) is not simply a tiny ornamental beetle, but also a potent natural pest controller. Adults and their larvae can eat over 100 aphids per day. That's quite some appetite! Another killer is the aptly named assassin bug. This *gogga* eats millipedes and other insects after rushing

A footbridge crosses the Mossel River beyond Kwaaiwater. Cape clawless otters are sometimes spotted here.

and stabbing the victim with its powerful beak. It then injects a fast-acting paralysing toxin into its prey.

In this phenomenal ecosystem, it is inspiring to watch the sunbirds sipping nectar from the drooping red tubes of ericas and to spot the dassies peering from their craggy burrows. The latter usually come out in social groups, especially around the Old Harbour and at Gearing's Point, to sun themselves in leisurely fashion on the rocks and feed on the surrounding plant life. If startled, they will freeze, immobile as statues, and remain so until they feel it is safe to make a dash for their lairs. Over time, they become quite tame and have been known to wander up Harbour Road to forage.

The Cliff Path, accessible from different points along the way, offers superb whale-watching vantage points and different scenic aspects of the coastline. Benches en route are ideal for resting and reflecting on the panoramic seascapes.

From the historic Windsor Hotel, the path curves at Gearing's Point, extending past the Old Harbour, towards Village Square, where it continues to uncoil towards The Marine hotel and its tidal pool, next to Bientang's Cave Restaurant. Further along, the scenery expands to include homes with enviable sea views. Meandering past wind-sculpted hedges and boulders, the path takes you above the coves stretching out towards the horizon, all the way down to Grotto Beach.

On a hot summer's day, you might set off along the Cliff Path in the direction of Kammabaai.

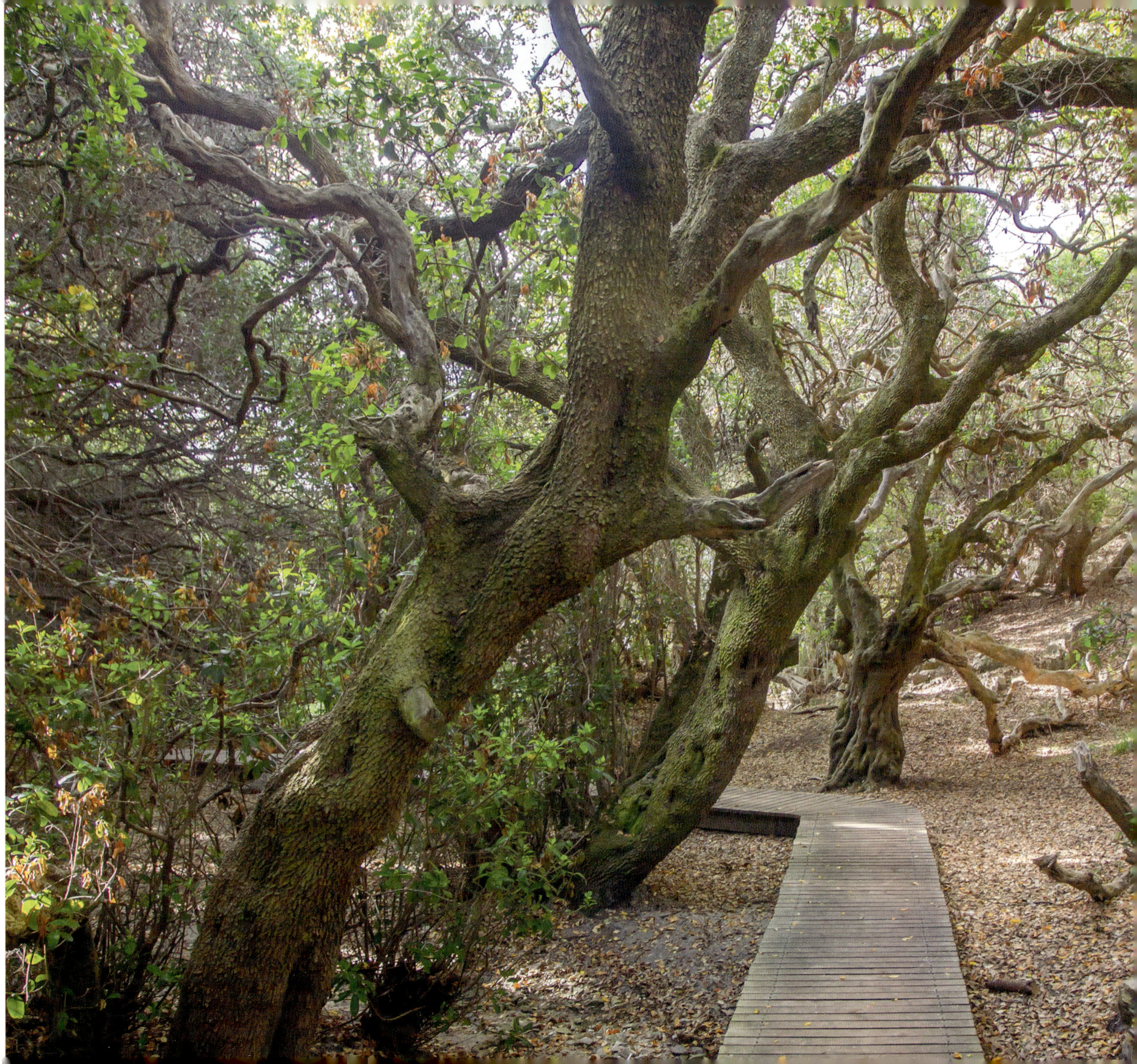

The milkwood forest known as Piet-se-Bos offers welcome protection from the sun on hot summer days. This shady glade can be reached from the Cliff Path or, alternatively, by following the network of paths from the parking area at Dutchies restaurant, opposite Grotto Beach, all the way to the lagoon.

HERMANUS 141

Early-morning walkers are greeted by a dazzling sunrise over Walker Bay (top). Other marvels encountered on the path include the indigenous pincushion (above left), grey-headed gulls (above centre) and cormorants (right).

BLOOD FLOWERS

Haemanthus coccineus or blood flowers (*bloedblomme*), so named because of their red flower and stem, pop up from the undergrowth along the Cliff Path. Common names for this perennial bulb are paintbrush, March flower and April fool, while in Afrikaans they are referred to as *rooikwas*, *bobbejaansool*, and *velskoenblaar* due to the shape of the leaves. The name *Haemanthus* is derived from the Greek words for blood and for flower; *coccineus* is the Latin word for red or scarlet. De L'Obel, a Flemish botanist, illustrated this species as far back as 1605 and it may well have been one of the very first South African flowers to have been featured in a European publication.

The Village News, March 2016

Fynbos and milkwood trees flank the path on either side. In some places the branches touch overhead to create umbrellas of shade. In this secret milkwood tunnel you walk alongside running streams winding among rocks covered with lichen, green ferns and lilies. Suddenly the glade of dappled sunlight breaks open into a Mediterranean vista, with the azure blue sea chasing white-tipped waves to the shore.

The roar of the ocean, the chorus of Christmas beetles, and the amazing views will lift your spirits to soar with the gulls above. It is a treat to head straight for the surf, plunging into the inviting coolness of the breakers rolling onto the beach.

On walks along the Cliff Path, you may see schools of dolphins rising in a spectacular acrobatic display through the waves. To witness this sleek dance sequence performed by the most gracious of marine mammals is an unforgettable experience.

Boiling Pot, at Gearing's Point, where rugged rock formations jut out into the sea, is a much-visited spot. Nearby, Castle Rock is a sundeck for cormorants, oystercatchers and gulls, and also a popular site for recreational anglers.

The rising tide in this tranquil coastal picture can unexpectedly turn into a 'boiling pot' of surging foam as it explodes in turbulent columns crashing down on the rocks, spawning a rush of water into the rocky gullies. After winter storms, witnessing the changing moods of the sea can be an invigorating experience. Sightseers gather on the rocky crescent with their digital cameras to catch amazing pictures!

A recent addition to the Cliff Path is a Solar System exhibit. The models of the planets have been built to scale and are dotted along the Cliff Path to Grotto Beach, spaced according to their distance from the sun in our solar system.

Rotary Way

'The creation of a thousand forests is in one acorn.'

Ralph Waldo Emerson

Rotary Way leads to some of the most magnificent views over Hermanus and its coastline. At the western entrance to town a tarred road, marked by a pair of signposted pillars, turns off the Mount Pleasant boundary and runs along the ridge of the Fernkloof Mountains.

Passing the outskirts of Mount Pleasant, the road winds its way around the hip of the mountain until you can see the undulating green slopes of the Hemel-en-Aarde Valley sprawling below.

Follow the road to the top where the vista expands in all directions to sweep over fynbos slopes, the entire length of the town and Walker Bay. This superb setting, high above Hermanus, is also the launching pad for hang-gliders and paragliders who create a colourful aero-display on a calm weekend day.

Beneath scudding clouds, Babylonstoren (meaning 'tower of Babel'), the highest peak in the Overberg, casts its shadow over the landscape. This peak reaches 1,168 metres above sea level and in winter is sometimes covered in snow, creating an Alpine vista.

Park your car at the end of the tarmac, and proceed on foot to the viewpoint where a bench invites you to rest and take in the scenery. Perhaps, through the echo of the gusting wind, you can still hear the distant murmur of the sea. What a picture you will see from this lofty natural grandstand, looking over the tree-lined streets and rooftops of the town, recognising Hoy's Koppie in the foreground and, way beyond, the sheer magnificence of the unbounded blue ocean! You can also see the Klein River Lagoon and the white sands of Grotto Beach stretching towards Gansbaai, as well as the beacon of Danger Point Lighthouse.

Now make your way up a stony path amid swathes of fynbos carpeting the slopes in pink and purple ericas, rising like natural bouquets out of the greenery. From here, unlimited views unfold to show the New Harbour and the coastal stretch of Vermont.

> ## Hermanus histories
>
> The building of this scenic drive was the inspiration of a man confined to a wheelchair, whose vision, shared with three friends, became a reality. A contribution of 100 pounds from the Rotary Club in 1960 started the road, which was completed with the help of the local municipality. Rotary Way is a feature of Hermanus and one of its greatest assets, visited by many who enjoy the scenery and spotting whales.
>
> S. J. du Toit, *Hermanus Stories I*, 2001

Launching from Rotary Way, a paraglider gets a bird's-eye view of Hermanus.

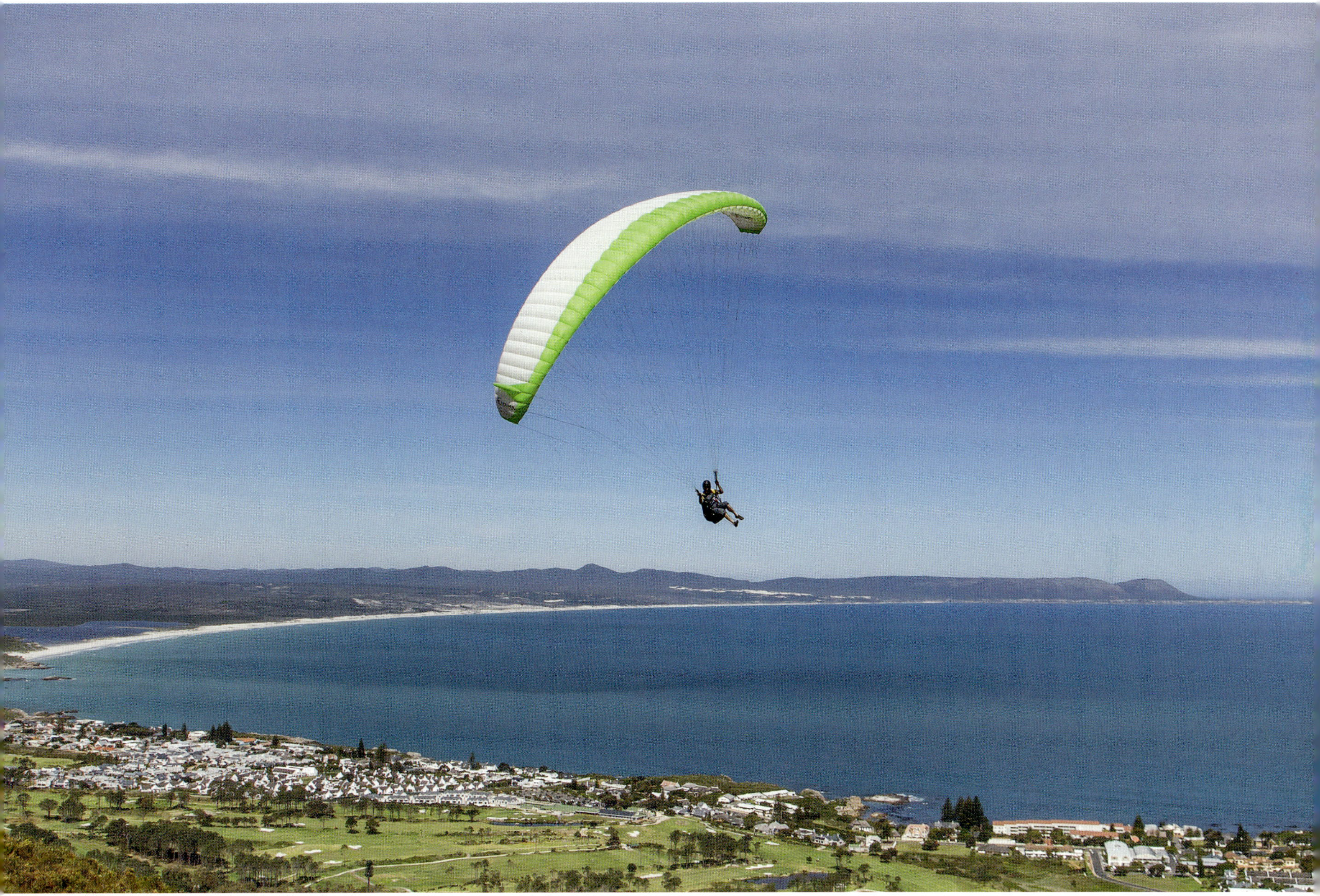

An array of walkways, hiking paths and cycling tracks crisscross Fernkloof Nature Reserve. There are more than 50 kilometres of hiking trails here, offering panoramic views across Walker Bay to the south and the Hemel-en-Aarde Valley to the west.

Pages 148–149: Some 1,500 species of fynbos, including several endemic plants, are found in Fernkloof.

Fernkloof Nature Reserve

'In every walk with nature one receives far more than he seeks.'

John Muir, *Travels in Alaska*, 1915

Escape from the high-tech demands and digital stresses of city life to a haven in the mountains where all the elements for serenity combine in a synthesis of nature's lush abundance. An estimated 1,500 species of fynbos grow on the slopes of the mountains in the Fernkloof Nature Reserve, famous for its fauna and flora. This indigenous fynbos biome is part of the Cape Floristic Region, one of only six in the world and by far the smallest but richest in number of species.

The Hermanus Botanical Society offers guided tours to view the proteas, ericas and other fascinating fynbos plant species that grow here. Peak flowering time is in spring (September and October), when the fynbos is at its best.

Way back in 1923, a well-respected and much-loved Hermanus schoolmaster, William Paterson (known as *Meester* Paterson), who had a passion and vast knowledge of Cape flora, took indigenous wild flowers to England, where they were much admired. During the flowering of the everlastings, Paterson would organise a team of as many as 40 harvesters in the mountains. One year he exported 13,000 pounds of dried everlastings to Germany. Master Paterson could often be seen on horseback, searching the slopes for new species. At least three are named after him: *Erica patersonia*, *Protea patersonia* and *Leucospermum patersonii*.

At the reserve, different plants blossom throughout the year, so there is always something to see. Many of the 42 protea species are a picture during the winter months (June, July and August). The fame of Fernkloof has brought ecotourists from all parts of the globe to explore the delights of these floral treasures on the Klein River Mountain slopes.

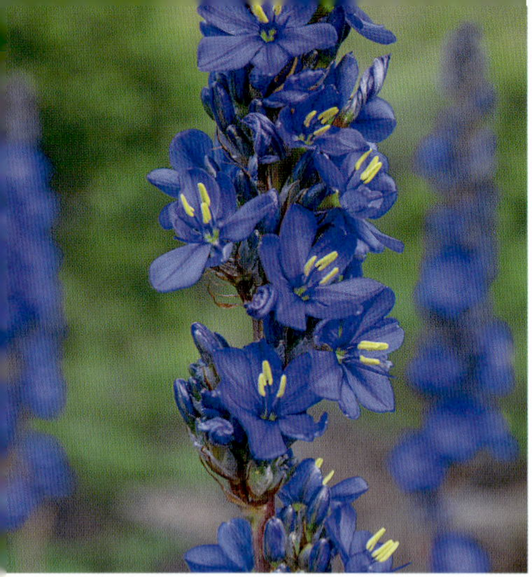
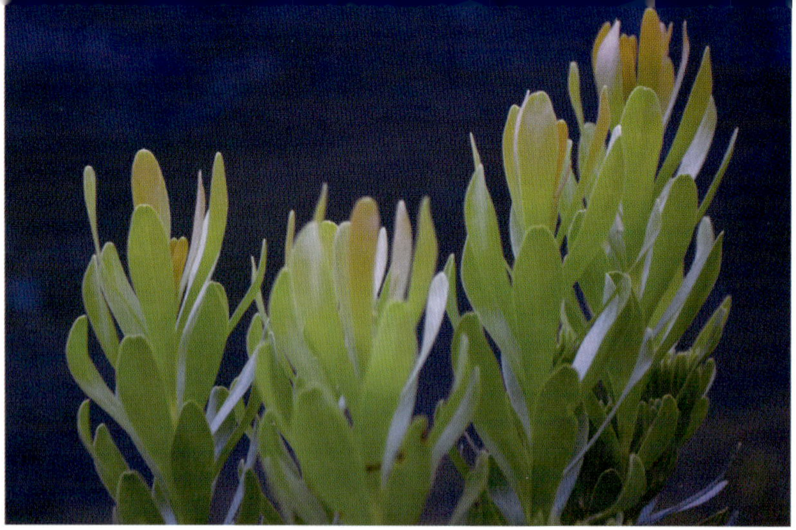
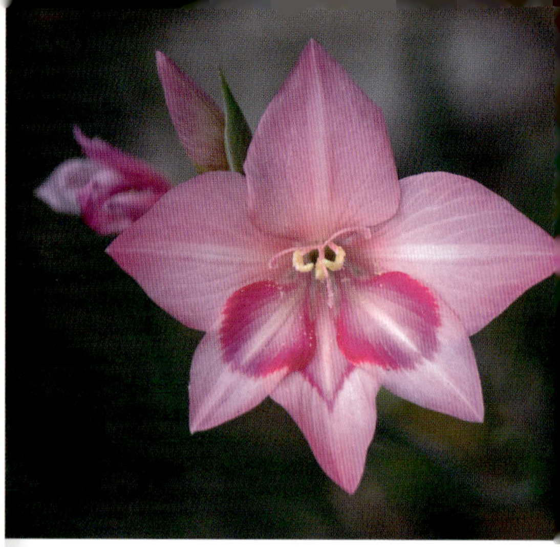
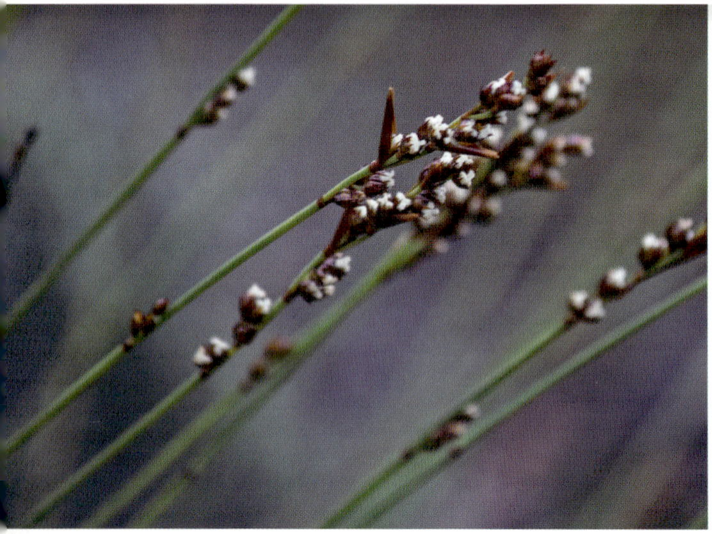
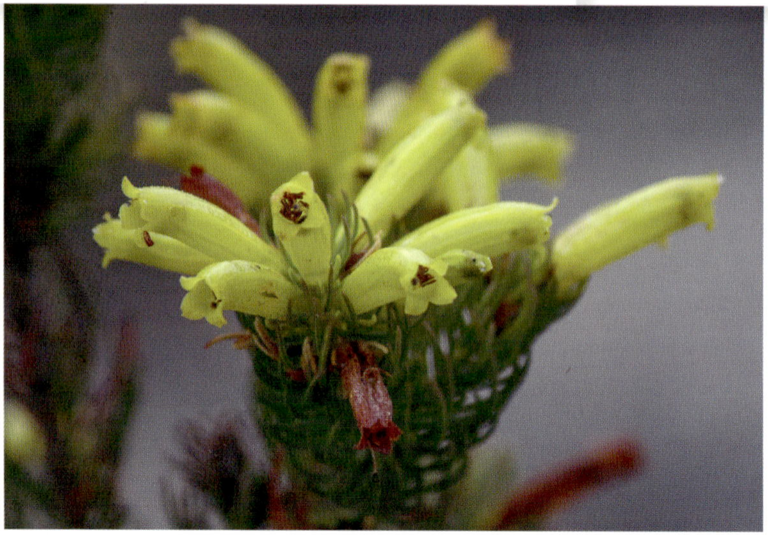
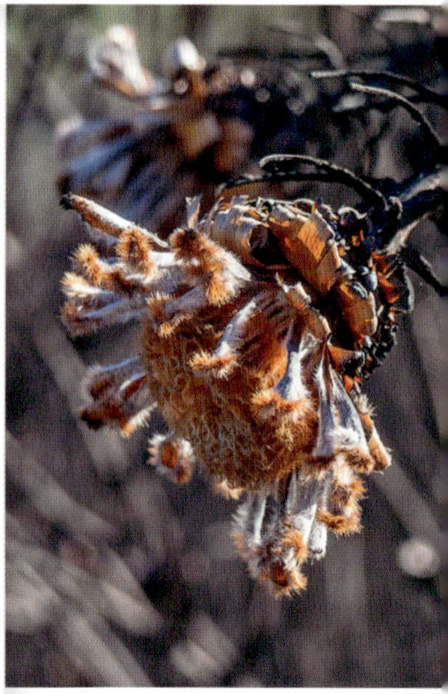
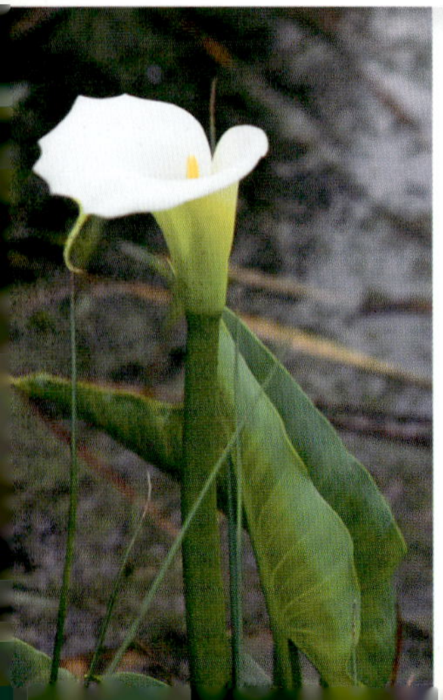
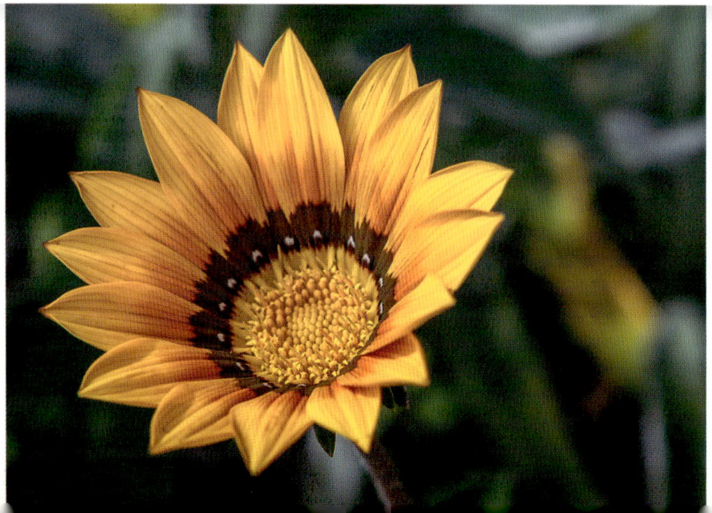
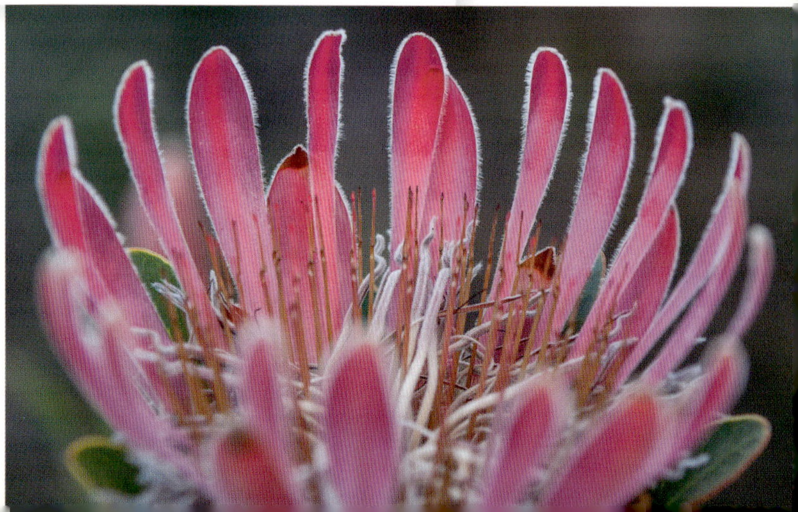

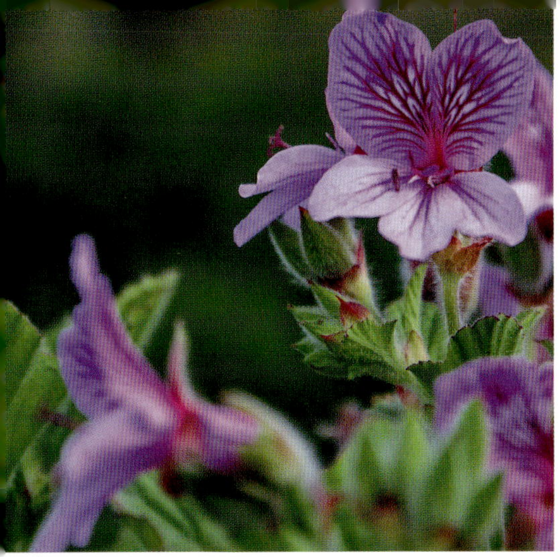
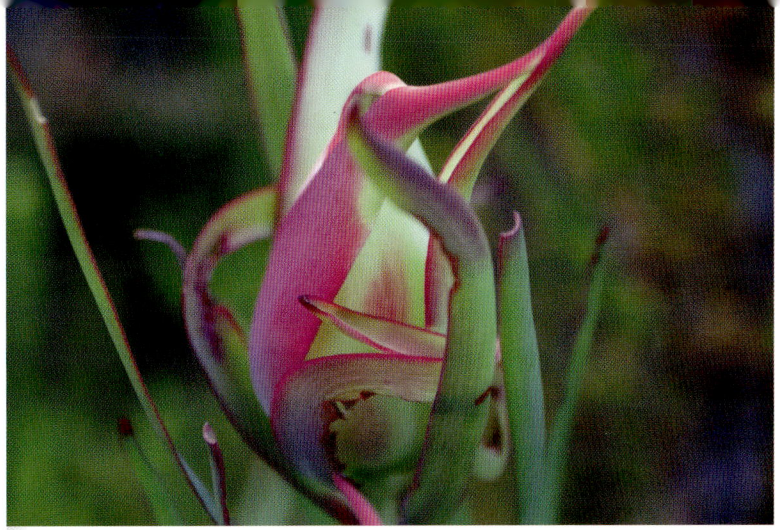
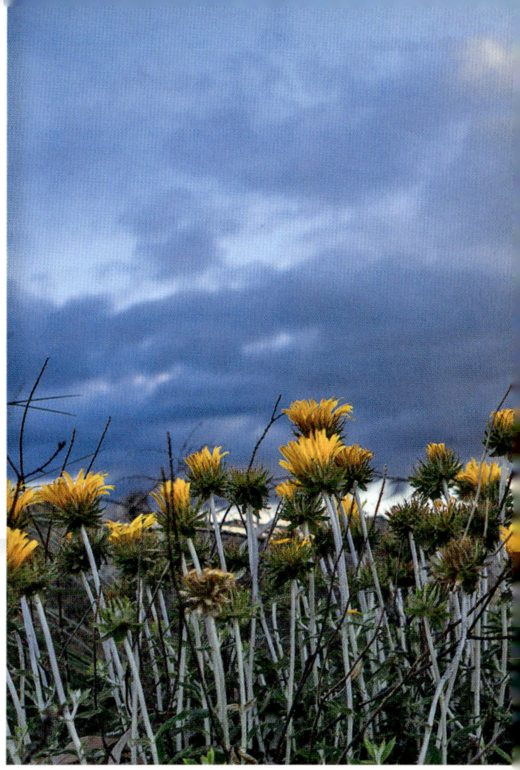
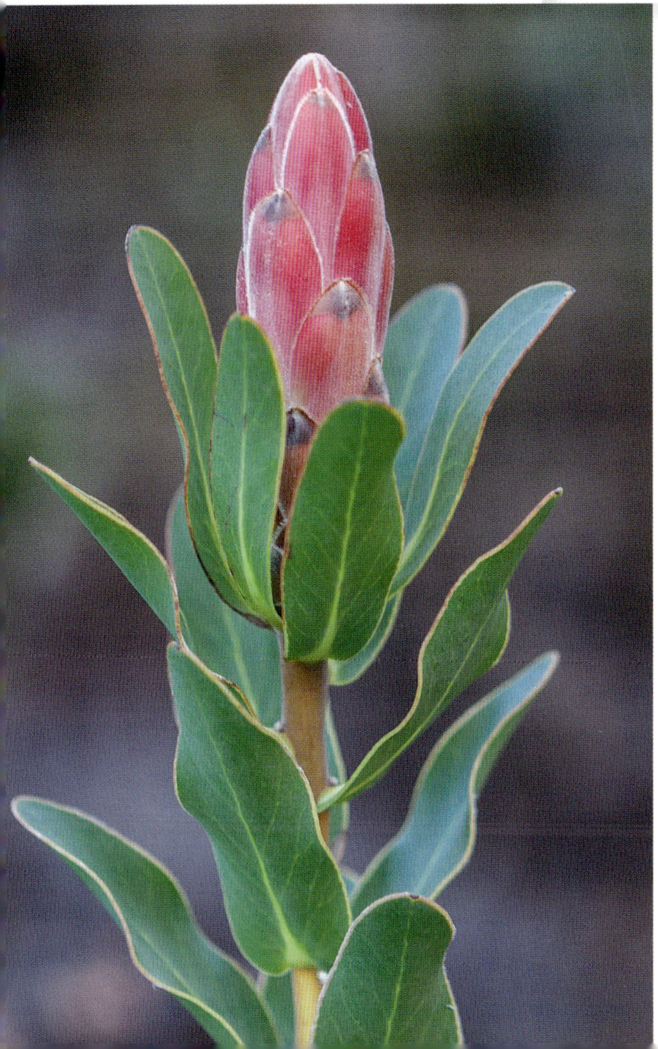
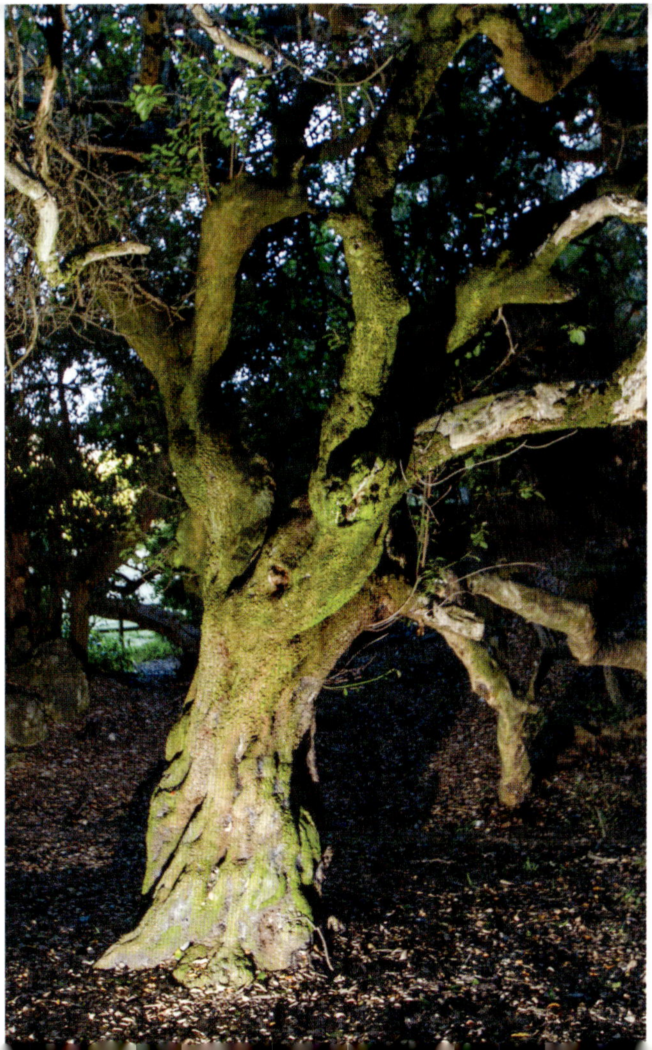
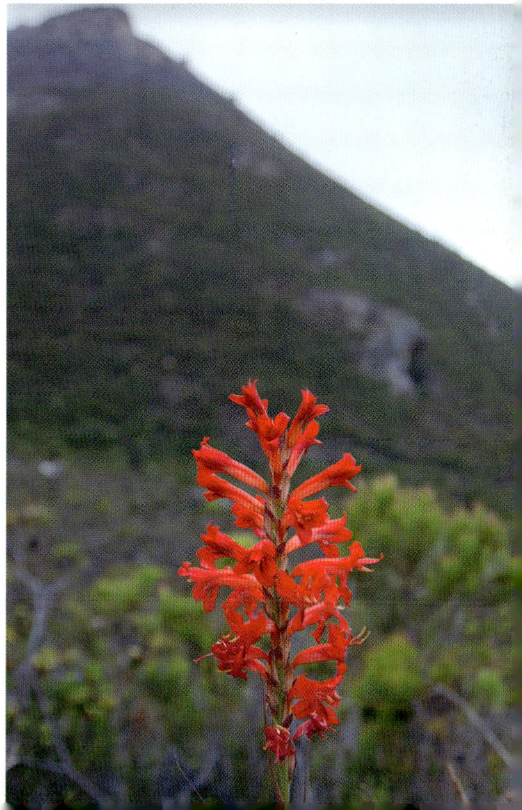

The various species of fynbos are exhibited at the Hermanus Herbarium at Fernkloof. In this cornucopia of botanical beauty, there are more species growing in close proximity than anywhere else in the world.

Another indigenous species was discovered in Fernkloof in March 2016. The *Disa forficaria*, an extremely scarce orchid, was last seen in 1966 near Houwhoek in the Elgin Valley. Prior to that it had only ever been seen half a dozen times. This is the first sighting of this species in the Fernkloof Nature Reserve. Such a rare find strongly emphasises the great value of the reserve and the ongoing need to protect it at all costs.

At the entrance to the reserve, a sign reads: 'Tortoises have the right of way'. The sign on the door of a hut nearby reads: 'Please keep closed because of the baboons'. Notices such as these epitomise the philosophy of the reserve. In a sensitive biosphere such as this, an awareness of nature conservation is a priority.

Apart from tortoises and baboons, the reserve is home to grey rhebok, klipspringers, Cape grysbok, steenbok, porcupines, dassies, mongooses, hares, skinks, lizards and nine species of snake. There are about 100 different bird species in the reserve, including the Cape sugarbird, rock thrush, Cape batis and ground woodpecker. Raptors such as Verreaux's eagle and jackal buzzard also occur here.

The Fernkloof Visitors' Centre also displays several plant species, with their identification and history. Extensive research is performed here on the rich diversity of plant life at Fernkloof.

Fynbos is characterised by four main growth forms, each having a distinctive shape and texture:
- reed-like plants such as restios and sedges
- small-leafed bushes such as ericas and buchus
- large-leafed woody shrubs like proteas and pincushions
- plants with underground storage organs (geophytes), such as watsonias and lachenalias.

Pick up a walking stick at the Visitors' Centre and make your way along the mountain slopes. Follow the meandering paths past the staggering stone structures reaching for the sky, and delight in a sense of outdoor adventure as you cross over streams on suspended wooden bridges.

All footpaths and trails are signposted. Perhaps you may choose to rest on a bench where rustic wooden arrows direct you to Lemoenkop, Boekenhoutbos and Three Dams. More ambitious visitors may decide to walk to the waterfall, or maybe go the whole way with a nature escape and stay overnight at Galpin Hut.

The nature reserve, encompassing about 2,000 hectares of mountain and coastal fynbos, has more than 50 kilometres of hiking trails. Part of the Hermanus Cycle Trail also traverses Fernkloof. Whether you are on foot or cycling, the expansive views over Walker Bay, the Hemel-en-Aarde Valley and Maanskynbaai ('moonshine bay') are exceptional.

Remember, when encountering any animals in the reserve, to be quiet and observe their movements. Give them the right of way, and never feed or leave food for any animal.

Vogelgat (meaning 'bird hole') is a private reserve adjoining Fernkloof and stretches all the way down to the Stanford road. In this sanctuary of breathtaking fauna and flora, small stone cottages have been built to provide overnight stays. A permit is necessary to visit the reserve.

The Overberg is a bird lover's paradise. Its different ecosystems of 'hotspots' in mountain, coastal, river and estuarine environments create a wide variety of habitats. Birds belonging to more than 330 species can be seen throughout the region.

In Hermanus the mountain escarpment and vegetation, and the close proximity to the sea and two large lagoons, create a natural avian reserve for a diversity of birds. Spot them on the Cliff Path, where over 60 species have been recorded, or take a trip to the bird sanctuary surrounding the Bot River Lagoon and the Afdaks River.

The 187 different species that inhabit this area include pelicans, sandpipers, spoonbills, herons, yellow-billed duck, coots, pied kingfishers, red bishops and many more. Sometimes flamingos, in an elegant pink flock, gather to sojourn in the shallows of the lagoon.

Opposite: A sign in Fernkloof Nature Reserve reminds motorists to slow down to avoid injuring the tortoises in this sanctuary.

Left: The Cape sugarbird is a common sight in Fernkloof as it flies from one protea to the next.

Blue cranes (left), South Africa's national bird, and spurfowls (above) are some of the species that can be spotted in the Overberg region.

The Overberg Birding Route provides an opportunity for ornithologists to experience the rich and diverse bird life of the southernmost region of Africa. South Africa's national bird, the endangered blue crane, inhabits the wheat fields and country pastures. In winter the cranes gather in large flocks on the farmlands. Breeding takes place in spring and summer. The blue crane mates for life and raises one or two chicks per year. These graceful birds, whether flying or flocking in fields, are a memorable sight. Their courting dance suggests classical ballet, and their haunting bugle-cry alerts you to look up as they fly overhead.

Cranes feed on various plants, insects and other small animals. At night they roost in the water to protect themselves and their chicks from predators.

The blue crane is an extremely sensitive species and is dependent on managed ecosystems for its preservation. Half of the remaining population is found in the Overberg area, where their numbers have increased dramatically due to the conservation efforts of the Overberg Blue Crane Group.

FLORAL SANCTUARY

Fernkloof Nature Reserve, established in 1957, lies at the extreme west end of the Klein River Mountains, which form part of the geological formation known as Table Mountain Sandstone. This was laid down in the sandy bed of a great sea about 400 million years ago. Flowering plants first appeared about 100–70 million years ago. The plants one now sees have survived in more or less the same form for millions of years.

Baboons

'Animals are such agreeable friends – they ask no questions, they pass no criticisms.'
George Eliot

The mountains around Hermanus are inhabited by troops of baboons. At night, they rest in kranses or high trees. They are omnivorous animals, very social and move around in small groups. Sometimes they come down from the slopes to explore the suburbs, and are often known to get up to mischief. Their 'monkey business' is seldom appreciated by the residents, who voice their ire in letters to the local newspaper.

The controversy about baboons gate-crashing suburban bliss and stepping over human-made boundaries draws a mixed bag of opinions. It is true that they can be a nuisance and cause havoc, but it is important to note that not only is this landscape their natural habitat, but also these primates play an important part in the fynbos ecosystem.

Baboons are a highly social species, and mostly active during the day.

Precious seeds are contained in baboon dung, thereby contributing to seed dispersal, while pollen sticking to their fur aids pollination. Though we may feel inconvenienced by baboons, their rights need to be taken into account − bear in mind that these primates roamed this coastal paradise long before humans arrived to peg out their territory.

Should you come across baboons while walking in the mountains, continue slowly on your way. Do not threaten them, corner them or feed them. In the unlikely event of a baboon behaving aggressively, move away slowly.

Baboons are a very intelligent, social species. Adult males can be recognised by a dark mane on the neck and shoulders. The females are the core of the group, and young males migrate to find a new troop when they are of age. Males fight for alpha status and can sometimes give baboons a bad reputation for being aggressive, which they are not under normal circumstances.

When the indigenous chacma baboons, also known as the *Kaapse bobbejaan*, come down the mountains to investigate how their cousins live, the results can be disconcerting. One resident, who came across three of them rearranging pots and pans in her kitchen and creating chaos in the fridge, took the sensible approach by installing a security gate to prevent any further break-ins.

The irreversible damage to the natural environment caused by human impact over hundreds of years has resulted in the significant shrinkage of natural habitats, causing wild animals to seek out resources in human-inhabited areas. This inevitably leads to conflict.

Opposite and above: As urban development increasingly encroaches on the natural habitat of baboons, conflict with humans becomes more likely. Efforts to manage baboon incursions into settled areas are under way in Hermanus.

A proposal to keep the baboons away from urban areas has been put forward by the company Human Wildlife Solutions (HWS), and is being implemented in the Hermanus area. This entails collaring the dominant male and female baboons of the troop with a sound box and tracking them via cellphones. Should the baboons get too close to town and threaten primate pandemonium in the suburbs, the sound box will be activated; the roar of predators, the sound of animals dying or in distress, and even small pyrotechnics that produce a loud bang will be employed to scare the baboons away if necessary. This 'virtual boundary' will identify the town to the baboons as a dangerous place to venture into. According to HWS, this is a humane way of moving baboons out of urban areas.

BABOON TALES

Approximately 250 baboons live in more than 12 groups in the Overstrand. The mountains behind Hermanus are home to three troops: the Fernkloof troop is usually active in Voëlklip; the Vogelgat troop can be seen en route to Stanford, and the Hamilton Russell troop lives in the Hemel-en-Aarde Valley ... Penalties for hunting baboons are up to two years in jail or a R10,000 fine, or both.

The Village News, September 2016

THE HEMEL-EN-AARDE VALLEY

'A winning combination of better viticulture, the development of new wine regions and the emergence of a young generation of wine-making talent make South Africa the most dynamic wine-producing country in the world right now.'

Tim Atkin, British wine master

One of the most scenic drives on the doorstep of Hermanus takes you into the Hemel-en-Aarde Valley. Beneath the slopes of the Glen Vauloch mountainside, vineyards cross-stitch the landscape in seasonal shades of summer greens or autumn russets.

Wine has been produced at the Cape ever since the first European settlers arrived here, and Constantia dessert wine enjoyed great fame in the early part of the last century. While vines thrived in areas like Paarl, Stellenbosch and Franschhoek, Hermanus, situated alongside the cold Atlantic Ocean, was not regarded as an area with any wine-growing potential. But that was before wine pioneer Timothy Hamilton Russell realised his vision of cultivating vines in Hemel-en-Aarde's verdant valley. Starting at grassroots in 1975 on an undeveloped 170-hectare farm, his entrepreneurial success and emergence as a leading player in the South African wine industry planted the seeds for the lavish mosaic of vineyards now seen in this region. In 1991 Anthony Hamilton Russell took over from his father, building on the estate's distinctive, original style made possible by the stony, clay-rich, shale-derived soil.

Right: As the seasons change, the vineyards at Newton Johnson begin their slow transformation from a summer palette of greens to the shades of russet that characterise autumn.

Above: The beautiful colour of Hamilton Russell's dark and spicy Pinot Noir.

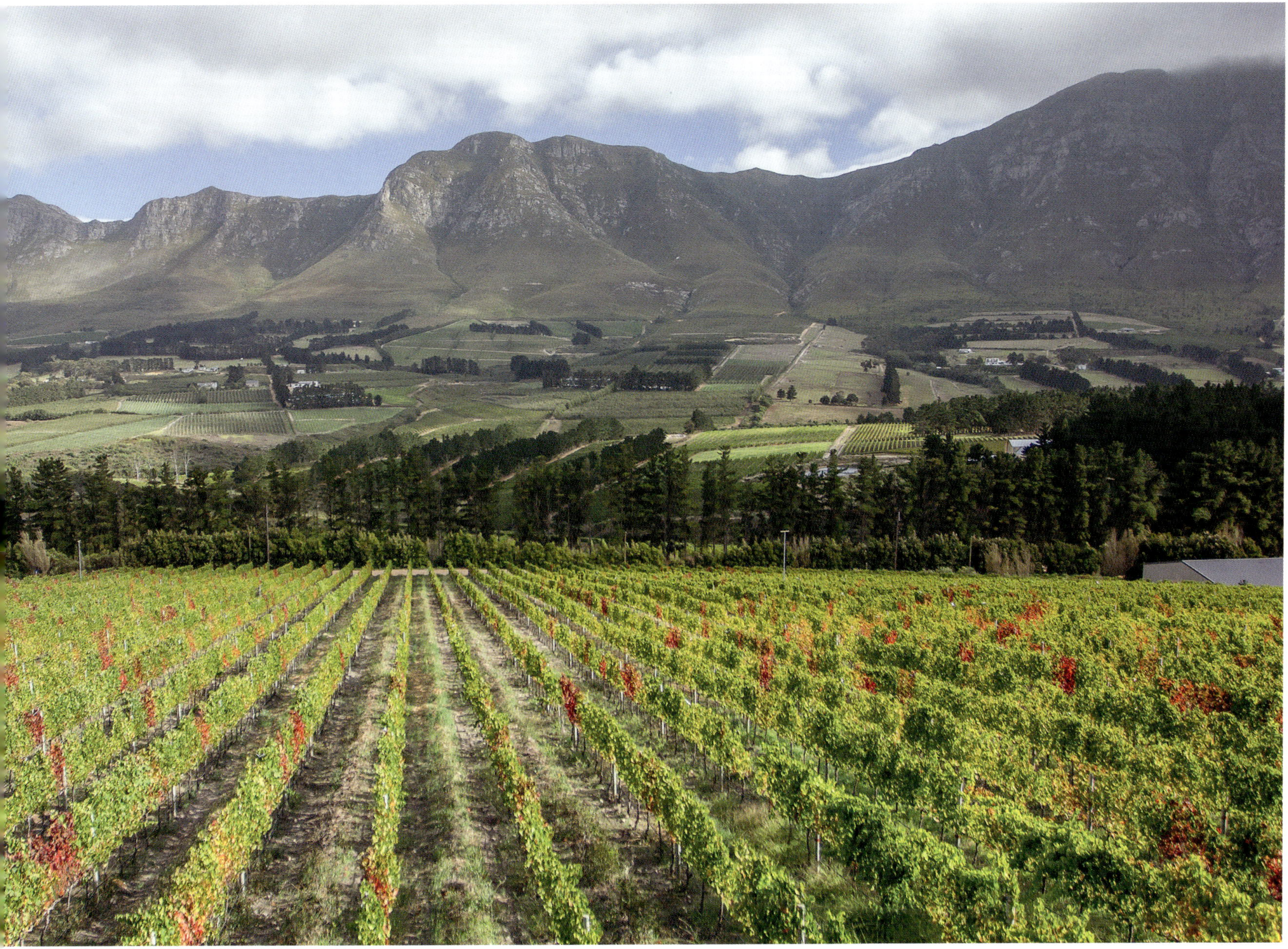

The R320 Wine Route

*'All wines should be tasted;
Some should only be sipped,
But with others, drink the whole bottle.'*

Paulo Coelho, *Brida*, 1990

The road through the Hemel-en-Aarde Valley may once have been the one 'less travelled', way back in the nineteenth century, when a toll was levied on horses, wagons and carriages entering the valley, but this is certainly no longer the case. Since Timothy Hamilton Russell's maverick move to this part of the world in 1975, which stimulated the expansion of viticulture in the Hemel-en-Aarde area, the Walker Bay Wine District's Route 320 has grown into a sought-after region that represents the best in estate wines that South Africa has to offer. On the R320, you will taste legendary Pinot Noirs as well as award-winning Chardonnays, some of the country's finest examples of Sauvignon Blanc and Shiraz, and a variety of innovative blends.

Blessed by Bacchus, this idyllic valley has just the right microclimate and combination of soils to make it ideally suited to the creation of award-winning wines. The welcome sea breezes keep the vines cool, thereby encouraging slow ripening and richly flavoured grapes. The Hemel-en-Aarde Valley seems to attract the *crème de la crème* of winemakers, not only those with local roots, but also those from further afield, who add a cosmopolitan feel to the area. It is also a first-class destination for local and international visitors, drawn to the region by its excellent cuisine and acclaimed wines.

Left: The Hermanus Wine Route is located along the R320, which winds its way through the picturesque Hemel-en-Aarde Valley between Hermanus and Caledon.

Opposite: The Hemel-en-Aarde Valley is renowned for the world-class wines produced by the valley's estates, which include (bottom, from left to right) Whalehaven, Hermanuspietersfontein and Bartho Eksteen Wines.

Respected and established wineries located in this premium wine region are featured below. For information as to which estates offer public wine tastings, visit www.overbergwine.com.

WHALEHAVEN
The name of this artisanal winery alludes to Walker Bay, the marine sanctuary that provides a safe haven for southern right whales. The Wine Experience Centre, with its handcrafted décor, offers, among many other attractions, private tastings in the Winemaker's Lab and various 'tasting boards' showcasing aromatic aspects of the wines. The winery is renowned for its award-winning Pinot Noir and Chardonnay.

HERMANUSPIETERSFONTEIN
Situated 250 metres from the Hemel-en-Aarde Valley entrance, this wine cellar is renowned for its impressive range of Sauvignon Blancs, Bordeaux, and Rhône-style blends. A trademark is the expressive Afrikaans names given to the wine brands − the only cellar in South Africa that does this. Look out for labels like *Posmeester* ('postmaster'), *Skoonma* ('mother-in-law'), *Bloos* ('blush'), and many more such creations at this 'proudly local' winery.

BARTHO EKSTEEN WINES AND WIJNSKOOL
Bartho Eksteen, the maestro winemaker widely known as Monsieur Sauvignon, was invited to become a member of the prestigious Cape Winemakers' Guild, a privilege acknowledging him as an expert in his field and crediting him for the significant role he plays in the development of the South African wine industry. According to Bartho, the goal of Wijnskool is to offer future

generations the wonders of the world of wine and, among other aspects of viticulture, to encourage a passion for the terroir, and to teach the love and nurturing with which the product is prepared. Bartho won the Diner's Club Winemaker of the Year Award in 2010 with his 2009 Sauvignon Blanc. He and his wife, Suné, offer wine tastings by appointment. They also prepare picnic baskets for those who would like to linger longer.

CRYSTALLUM

This small, family-run winery is privately owned by the brothers Andrew and Peter-Allan Finlayson – the third generation of Finlayson winemakers and the sons of the man who pioneered the making of Pinot Noir in the Hemel-en-Aarde Valley and in South Africa. At Crystallum the brothers seek to produce classic wines, combining fruit sourced from new-world vineyards with a traditional, age-old way of working. The only varieties that they work with are Pinot Noir and Chardonnay, with multi-vineyard blends and single-vineyard wines making up the collection. Crystallum was founded in 2007 and had a first production of only 4,134 bottles of Sauvignon Blanc. In 2008 they introduced Pinot Noir and Chardonnay to the portfolio, and today Crystallum is exclusively producing these Burgundian varieties.

SOUTHERN RIGHT

The boutique vintner Southern Right, co-owned by Anthony and Olive Hamilton Russell, produces a serious and age-worthy Pinotage (South Africa's unique red grape variety), creating a distinct South African fruit and flavour expression with classic styling and refinement. The vineyard's Sauvignon Blanc is a local and international bestseller, with its classic, tight minerality complementing the prominent varietal fruit. The labels of their popular range of Pinotage and Sauvignon Blanc wines depict their namesake, the southern right whale. A portion of the proceeds of the wine sales goes to the conservation of Walker Bay's whales. Southern Right also has an ecological landscape of 200 hectares of fynbos, which forms part of a private nature reserve.

HAMILTON RUSSELL VINEYARDS

One of the most southerly wine estates in South Africa, and one of the closest to the sea, is Hamilton Russell Vineyards. This prestigious estate specialises in two highly acclaimed cultivars: Pinot Noir and Chardonnay. The elegance and highly individualised style of these terroir-driven wines can be appreciated from the tasting room terrace overlooking the dam. Hamilton Russell Vineyards has an enduring international reputation for quality and unusually classic styling. The estate's cultivars are widely regarded as among the best in South Africa and among the finest in the world. Hamilton Russell Vineyards uses large clay amphorae for maturing wines. In this way, the wine is matured in the same clay in which the vines grew. As *Platter's Wine Guide* puts it: 'You don't get much closer to the idea of "terroir" than that.' Hamilton Russell Vineyards is increasingly focused on organic cultivation. For the fifth time, in 2015, one of its wines was placed on the esteemed Wine Spectator Top 100 Wines of the Year worldwide list.

ASHBOURNE

Anthony Hamilton Russell decided in 1991 to produce a world-class wine without the traditional Bordeaux grape varietals, to craft something original and prevent comparisons. Accordingly, Ashbourne, a new vineyard site, was created. This 113-hectare property is farmed separately, and lies on the eastern border of Hamilton Russell Vineyards. The initial Ashbourne Red was soon followed by a white, the Sandstone, named after the soils in which the grapes are grown. The red is a Pinotage-based blend and the white is a Bordeaux white blend. Both elegant blends tend to lean towards the old-world style.

BOUCHARD FINLAYSON

Peter Finlayson's iconic wine, the Galpin Peak Pinot Noir, is the flagship product of this celebrated viticulturist and winemaker. Peter, who was initially based at Hamilton Russell Vineyards, is a pioneer winemaker of the Hemel-en-Aarde Valley. In 1989 he joined forces with Paul Bouchard, who hails from Burgundy, and the Bouchard Finlayson winery was opened on a 125-hectare property in the valley. In the cellar, Peter's superb winemaking has resulted in a variety of Pinot Noir, Sauvignon Blanc, Chardonnay and a dry white blend, Blanc de Mer, as well as hearty reds.

The wines created from the picturesque vineyards at Bouchard Finlayson (above, left and right) can be sampled at the estate's tasting room (top).

A large part of this estate is mountainous terrain, covered in spectacular fynbos. With only a small portion of the farm under vine, Bouchard Finlayson is able to ensure the conservation of the mountain land. At this wine estate, one can also opt for a fynbos trail hike with a choice of guided or self-guided walks and a selection of three different routes.

Bouchard Finlayson contributes to the Hermanus Rainbow Trust, which helps to provide children with basic education.

LA VIERGE PRIVATE CELLAR

La Vierge ('the virgin') was named for the virgin soil on which the farm was established. Although the estate is a specialist producer of Pinot Noir, it also makes Bordeaux and Rhône-style blends, Shiraz, Riesling, Sauvignon Blanc and Chardonnay. You will recognise the wines of this cellar by their creative and evocative labels sourced from history, biblical stories, myths and legends. Examples are: Seduction Pinot Noir, Nymphomane Cabernet, Jezebelle Chardonnay, and Last Temptation Riesling. The spectacular setting of the wine farm's restaurant and champagne terrace enhances the top-of-the-world gastronomic experience. It feels as if you are in the clouds as you take in the sweeping vistas across the valley below.

SUMARIDGE ESTATE WINES

This superb estate, owned by the Bellingham Turner family, lies between two majestic mountain ranges. Apart from the valley's earliest pioneers, this is one of the longest established producers in the area. From the winery you can take in views of the Atlantic Ocean, the source of the valley's cool maritime climate. The weather conditions are responsible for the exquisitely balanced wines produced at Sumaridge, such as Chardonnay, Sauvignon Blanc, Merlot, Pinot Noir, Pinotage, Syrah and Wayfarer Cap

The harvests derived from La Vierge's vineyards in the Hemel-en-Aarde Ridge appellation (top) eventually find their way into the cellar (above), where the wines are matured in French oak wine barrels.

Sumaridge provides a beautiful setting for outdoor concerts and events.

Classique. All the grapes for wine made on this estate are grown on Sumaridge soil, making each bottle an authentic 'estate' wine. In these beautiful surroundings, which also feature a trout dam, you can enjoy a lunch platter, and once the sun is over the yardarm, a special sundowner wine bar service is available.

Sumaridge supports and promotes local artists by making available a platform on the estate for showcasing the diverse range of talent in Hermanus as well as from further afield.

NEWTON JOHNSON FAMILY VINEYARDS

This wine farm was founded by Dave Johnson and wife Felicity (née Newton) in the mid-1990s. In their drive for high-quality yields, where assiduous, meticulous and creative work in cellar and vineyard is the goal, the emphasis is on natural processes – for example, the estate has chosen to use gravity rather than mechanical pumping, and to avoid yeast inoculation. Brothers Bevan and Gordon of the Newton Johnson family have created a state-of-the-art wine cellar. It is situated on a mountain slope in the

The family-run Newton Johnson Vineyards in the Upper Hemel-en-Aarde Valley is renowned for its Pinot Noir wines.

HERMANUS 163

Upper Hemel-en-Aarde Valley and has superb views of the valley and ocean. This family-owned winery is no stranger to accolades, having been the recipient of five stars in *Platter's Wine Guide* for every single vintage of Newton Johnson Family Vineyards Pinot Noir since 2009. These eight five-star vintages represent an extraordinary track record, unmatched by any other producer.

RESTLESS RIVER

The owners of this boutique winery, Craig and Anne Wessels, handcraft site-expressive wines from vineyards farmed as naturally as possible to develop depth and complexity. The estate has some of the oldest Cabernet Sauvignon and Chardonnay vineyards in the valley. Their acclaimed wines have their own distinctive character, shaped by the conditions of each year's vintage.

SPOOKFONTEIN

This hands-on winery, with its superb views and its landscape of vines, fynbos and olive trees, practises organic farming methods in order to create boutique products: single-vineyard Merlot, Cabernet Franc and Cabernet Sauvignon, as well as a blend, The Phantom. The winery keeps its winemaking style simple and true to the character of the land and soil.

Adjacent to the winery is Spookfontein Restaurant, which offers lunch and wine tasting.

ATARAXIA

The Greek name of this boutique wine estate denotes calmness and a tranquil state of mind. The vines are nurtured in a unique terroir created by the maritime climate and the convoluted

The modern tasting room and restaurant at Spookfontein was designed to blend in with the surrounding countryside.

The chapel-like tasting room at Ataraxia.

foothills that flank the valley. Wines are handcrafted to reflect the origin, elegance and sense of the place. Ataraxia's range includes Sauvignon Blanc, Pinot Noir, Chardonnay and a red blend. The wine lounge, built at the foot of the majestic Babylonstoren Mountains, resembles a chapel. It has spectacular views, making wine tasting here a sensual and memorable experience.

CREATION

Established in 2002, Creation is located on the Hemel-en-Aarde Ridge, at the furthest end of the R320 Wine Route. This innovative estate has garnered an impressive list of awards. In the Tasting Room there is a choice of no fewer than eight exciting pairing options. The wines of Creation are: Semillon, Viognier, Chardonnay, Pinot Noir, Reserve Pinot Noir, Merlot, Reserve Merlot, Syrah, Syrah-Grenache and Merlot-Cabernet Sauvignon-Petit Verdot. Tours of the vineyards and cellar take in the beauty of the surrounding fynbos gardens and displays of contemporary art — all of which contribute to the image of a distinctive wine range, created for those who enjoy the finer things in life.

DE BOS FAMILY VINEYARDS

With one of the pre-eminent vine nurseries in the southern hemisphere and three different growing regions from which to select their blends, the Bosman Family Vineyards have many options in

Acclaimed wines and contemporary art can be enjoyed at Creation.

HERMANUS 165

WINE VILLAGE

A one-of-its-kind, specialist wine shop, situated close to the vineyards and cellars on the R320 Wine Route, Wine Village pops a five-star cork in marketing the largest and finest selection of South African wines under one roof. But Wine Village is not just about wine – also on offer is a choice of craft beer, gin, brandy and whisky. The innovative owners, Paul and Cathy du Toit, both started their careers at KWV (a marketer and distributor of high-quality wine and spirits) in Worcester before realising their vision by creating a stylish library of quality brands at the foot of the Hemel-en-Aarde Valley.

In a plush classic cellar ambience you will find more than 6,000 different labels of wine, craft beer, Cap Classique, gin and brandy. Wine enthusiasts from near and far visit the Du Toits' renowned emporium to sample their superb selection of cultivars. This unique retail outlet distributes wine for clients locally and abroad and is open seven days a week, offering daily wine and olive tastings.

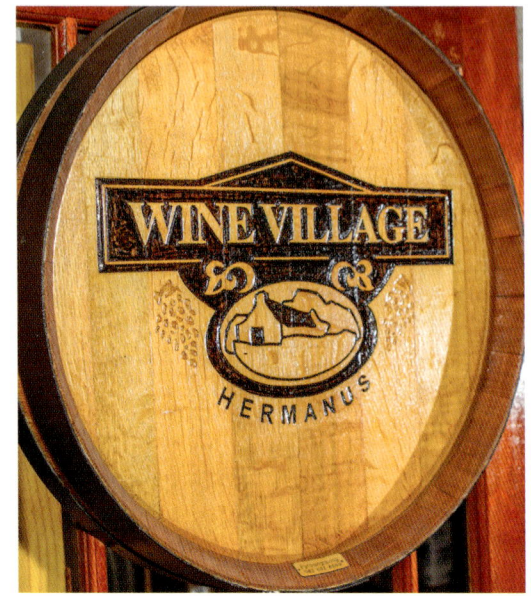

applying their expertise when it comes to crafting their wines. A strict selection process in the vineyard and the cellar means that only the top five percent of the total harvest is used for production. While historic vines offer distinct vintages, a thriving vine garden allows for constant innovation and the perfect blend of old and new.

MOUNT BABYLON

Established in 2001, Mount Babylon is a family-owned wine business situated amid fynbos and bird life in the foothills of the Babylonstoren Mountains. Having planted its first vines in 2001, Mount Babylon was the first wine farm in the cool Hemel-en-Aarde Ridge ward to venture into grape growing. This pioneering estate was also the first in the ward to obtain a four-star Platter rating for a red blend, namely its maiden vintage, SMV. This is now Mount Babylon's flagship wine, a blend unique in South Africa consisting of Shiraz, Malbec and Viognier. The 2007 contrarian Cap Classique is another popular Mount Babylon innovation, made from Shiraz grapes, rather than Pinot Noir and Chardonnay.

JAKOB'S VINEYARD

Against the slopes of Babylonstoren, this small family-owned vineyard and winemaking concern strives to create site-specific wines. Owners André and Yvonne de Lange focus on the principles of passion, excellence and simplicity in the crafting of their wines. Inspired by the unique confluence of art and science in the making and appreciation of fine wine, André, an attorney by profession, dreamed from an early age of making his own wine.

DOMAINE DES DIEUX

Domaine des Dieux ('domain of the gods') is situated on the Hemel-en-Aarde Ridge mountain range. Cultivars are carefully chosen to suite the terroir, with Pinot Noir, Chardonnay, Sauvignon Blanc, Syrah, Mourvèdre and red Rhône and Italian varietals grown here. From these grapes, limited volumes of seven award-winning premium wines are produced. A tasting room and champagne deck are set in the vineyards, and there is also a picnic terrace.

SEVEN SPRINGS VINEYARD

This is a premium wine producer whose vineyard nestles between Shaws Mountain to the north and the Teslaarsdal mountain range to the south. The oceanic influence, coupled with the soils derived from the local Bokkeveld Shale, gives the vines the potential to produce exceptional grapes that include Chardonnay, Sauvignon Blanc, Syrah and Pinot Noir.

STORM WINES

After ten vintages at Hamilton Russell Vineyards in the Hemel-en-Aarde Valley, winemaker Hannes Storm discovered two small parcels of land with particularly exceptional terroirs: one in the Hemel-en-Aarde Valley, characterised by low-vigour, stony, clay-rich shale soils, and the other in the Upper Hemel-en-Aarde Valley, typified by soils consisting of decomposed granite.

Since its maiden vintage in 2012, Storm Wines has crafted two superb Pinot Noirs and a Chardonnay from the vineyards planted in these wards – steering the purest characteristics of each site towards bottle and cork. A third Pinot Noir, added to the Storm stable in 2015, is made from vineyards grown in the Hemel-en-Aarde Ridge appellation. Storm Wines is the only producer to handcraft a Pinot Noir from each of the three appellations in the Hemel-en-Aarde Valley.

Small production, careful viticulture, minimal intervention in the cellar and a constant nod to the Old World give these wines their distinctive personality and character.

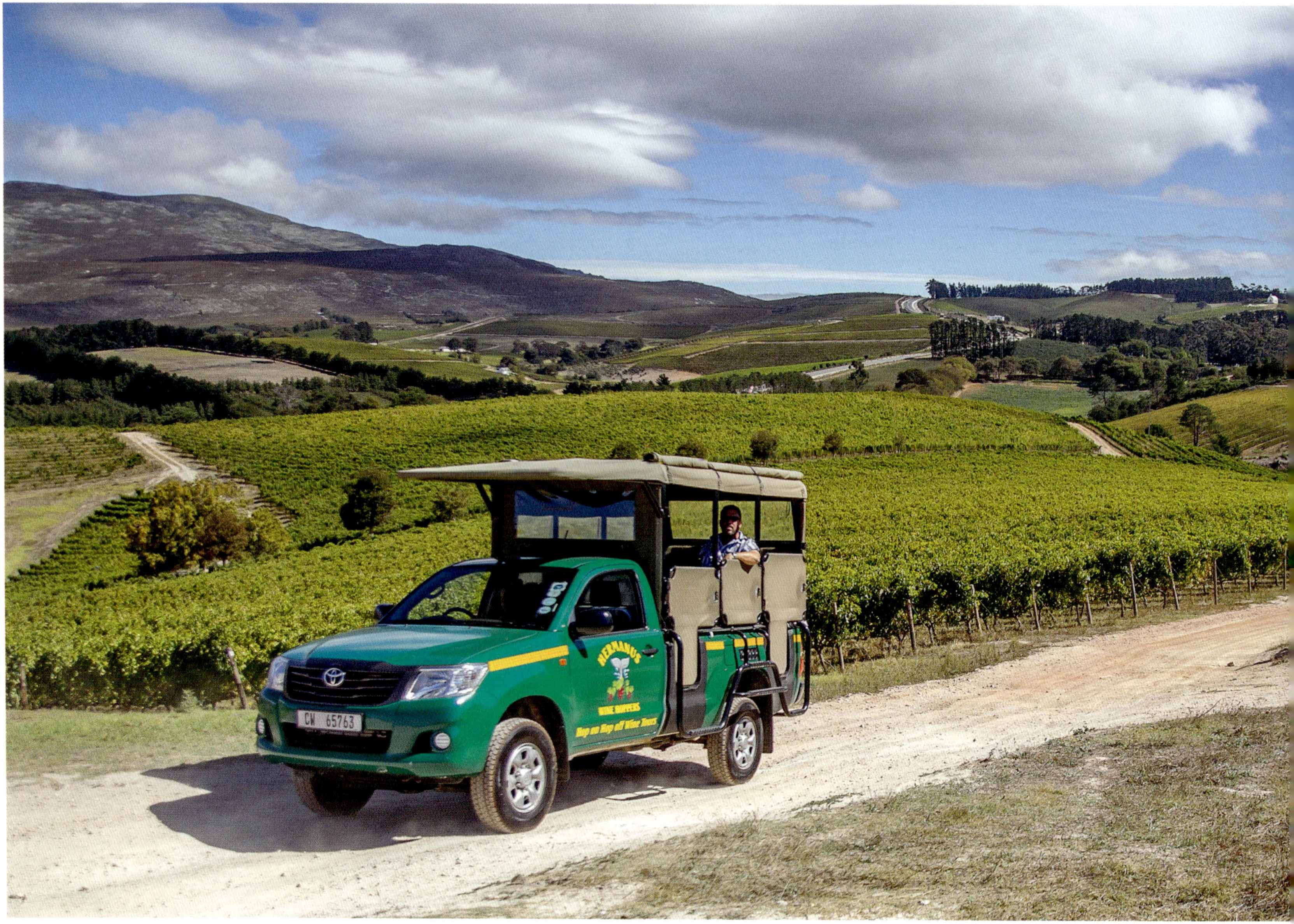
HERMANUS
CW 65763

HERMANUS WINE HOPPERS

Adding enjoyment to the wine route experience is Hermanus Wine Hoppers. This unique safari-style wine tour offers you a relaxed experience in comfort and safety. The greatest advantage of this hop-on hop-off service is that everyone can enjoy their wine-tasting adventure on the right side of the law, leaving no one with sour grapes! From the selection on offer it's up to each group of customers to choose which wine farms they want to visit. Thanks to the removable canopies on the safari vehicles, no matter what the forecast, it's always perfect Wine Hopper weather.

A typical 'wine safari' begins at the Wine Hoppers head office in the CBD. Let us suppose that you have chosen to start at Hermanuspietersfontein. Here the tasting experience will begin in earnest. Along with the wine, you will be enlightened about its origins and development – from the science of viticulture to the bottled product. Clearly, there's far more to a fermented grape than meets the eye! The master sommelier will tell you that the process of making a good wine has five basic components: harvesting, crushing and pressing, fermentation, clarification and ageing, and bottling. The challenge for avant-garde winemakers is to add variations along the way to ensure a unique quality in their cultivars.

Next to welcome you might be Whalehaven, whose cool and spacious wine experience centre is just a stone's throw down the road from Hermanuspietersfontein. Here the consultant's informative presentation may be followed by a wine and food pairing of superb cultivars balanced with handcrafted artisanal chocolate and botanical jams – a truly memorable occasion that harmonises culinary creations with the heady romance of the vine!

Back on board the green-and-yellow safari vehicle, you'll be heading further up into the verdant folds of the valley. A drive through the quilted vines on either side of the road could deposit you at the boutique winery of Bouchard Finlayson. This classic cellar under thatch exudes an air of antiquity. You might even imagine that you're hearing Gregorian chants delivered by robed monks among the barrels of traditionally aged wooded wines.

Just a few wine farms is enough for a single day – but there are many more to see. Plan another safari!

Left: Hermanus Wine Hoppers provides hop-on hop-off tours, taking visitors to, and collecting them from, their chosen wine estates in the Hemel-en-Aarde Valley.
Pages 170–171: The Hermanus Wine Route offers visitors a diverse selection of renowned and award-winning wines.

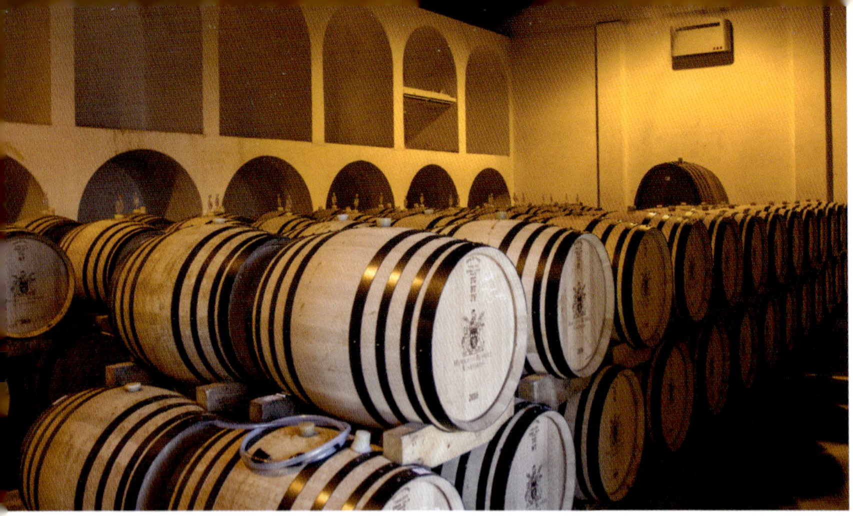
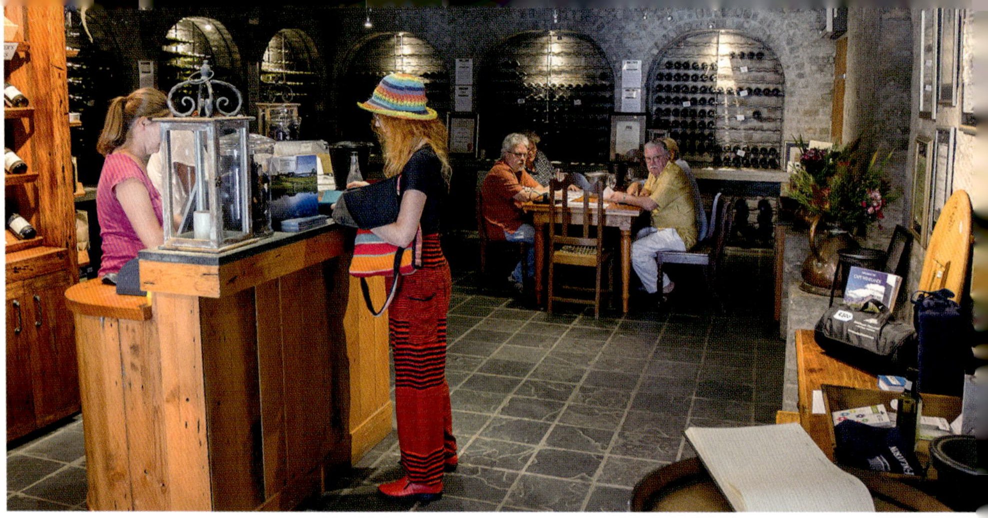
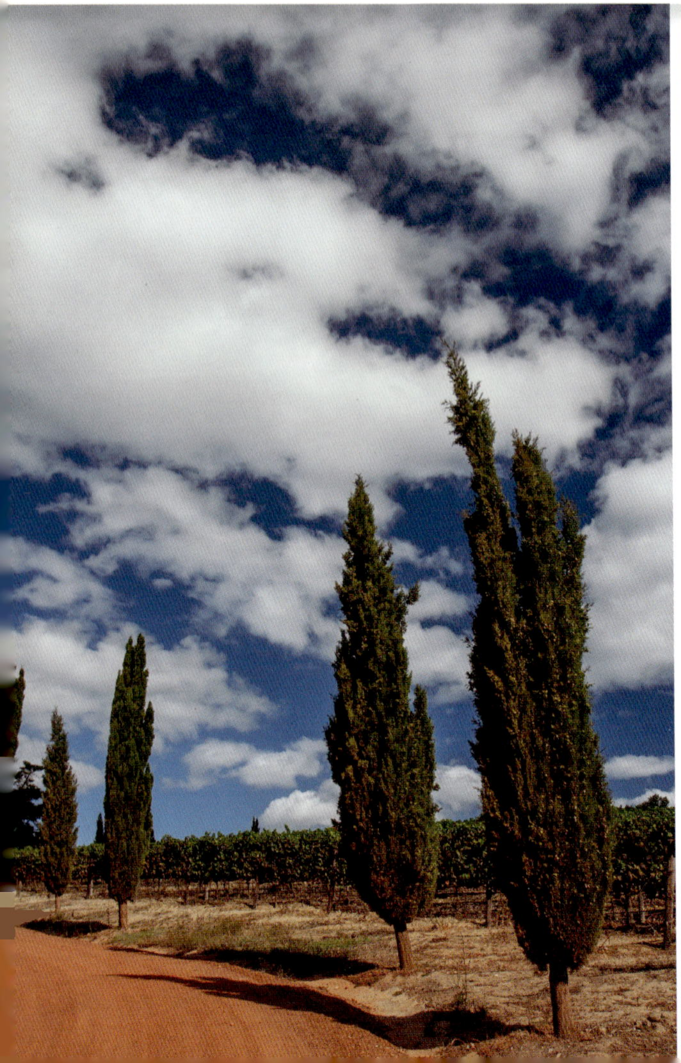
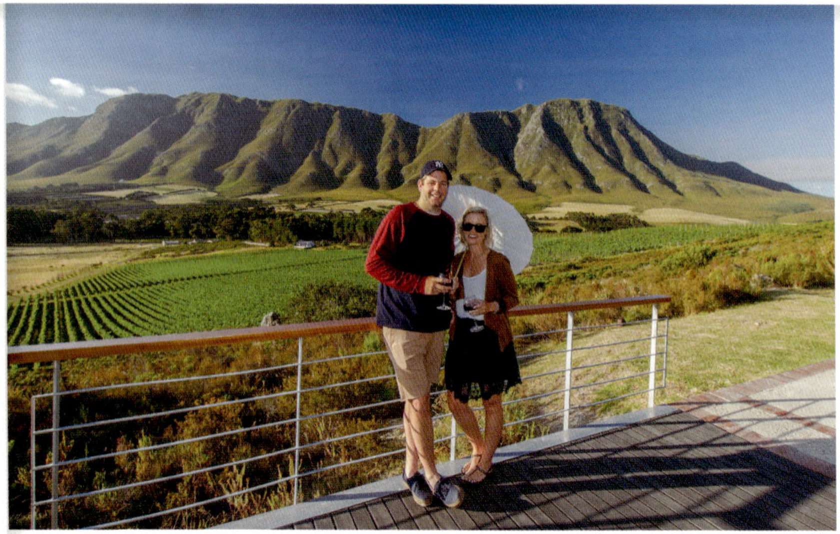
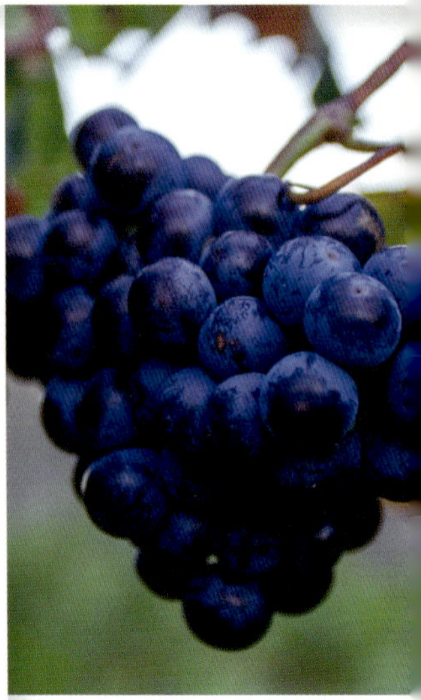
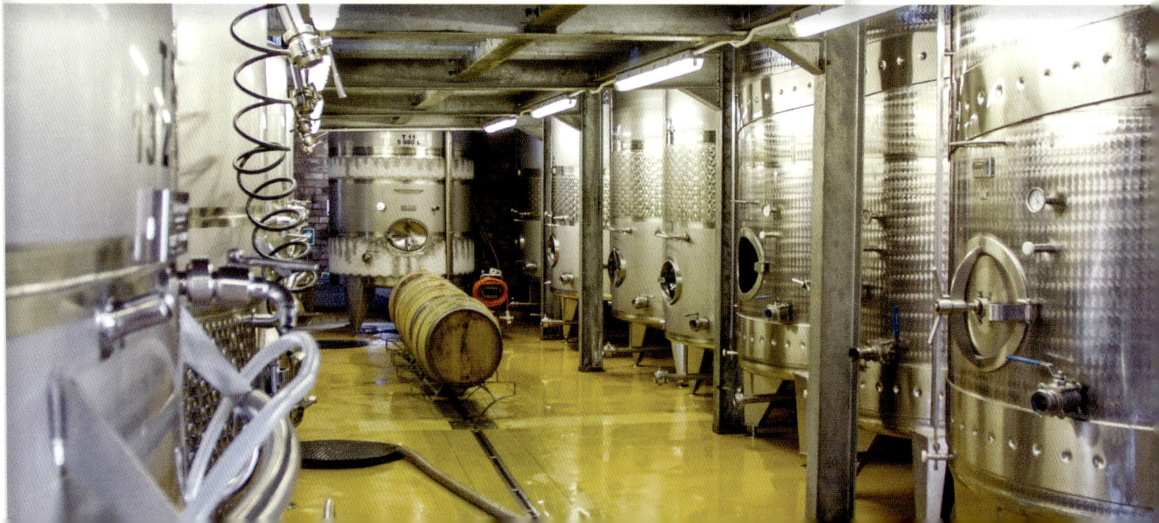

EXPORTERS
of
Cape
WINE VILLAGE
HERMANUS
For the finest selection of
A MEAL
without
WINE

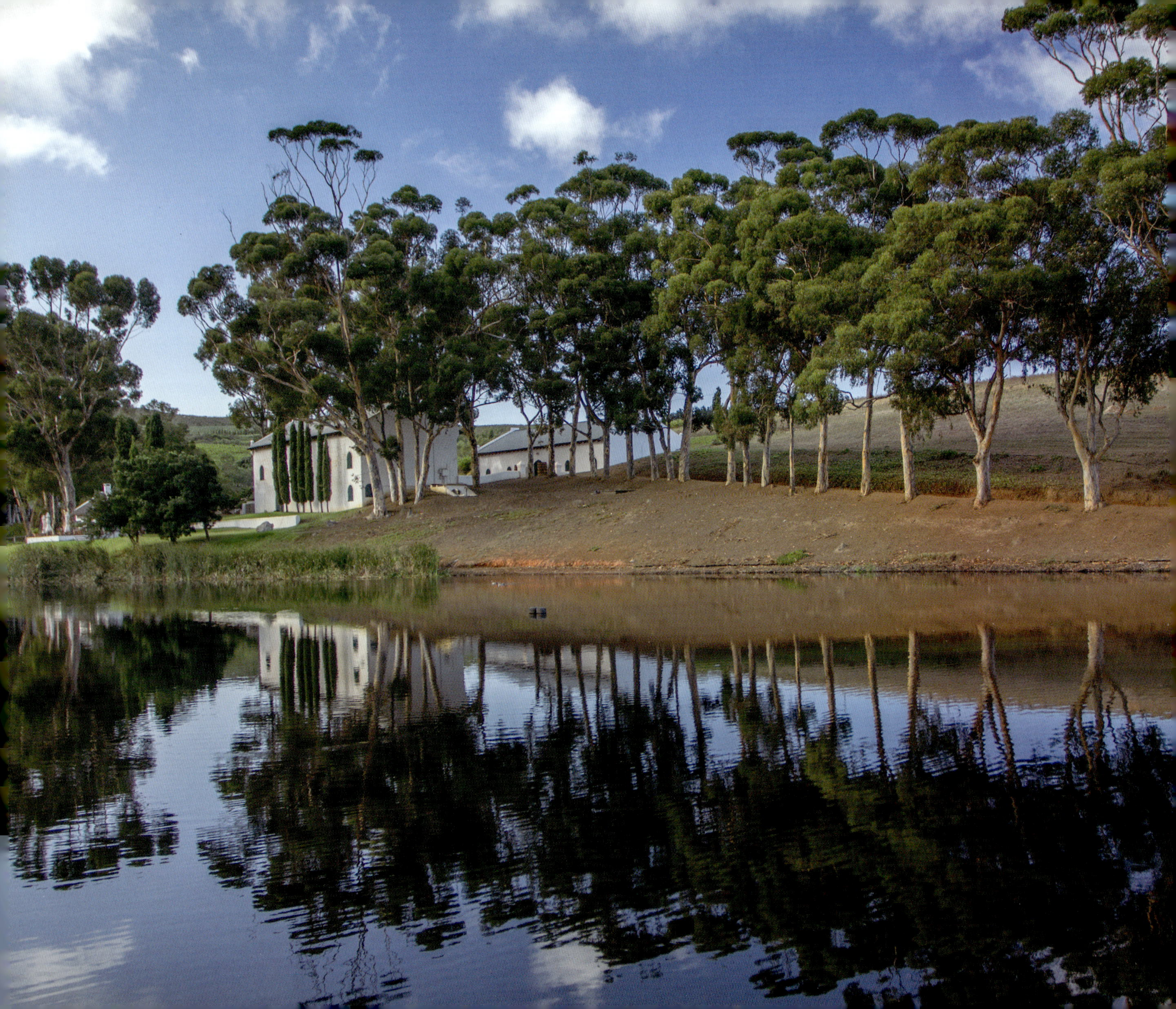

This heavenly landscape

'Live as though heaven is on earth.'
Anonymous

The Hemel-en-Aarde Valley is an idyllic cornucopia of natural assets. In this place of abundance, the yield of the grape is complemented by fresh produce, organic fare, cheeses and other handcrafted delicacies, as well as fruit farms, stud farms and superb restaurants, set amid lush green pastures, fields of lavender and olive groves.

The valley boasts more than just its vast array of wine farms. It is also famous for its superb restaurants, delis and stalls, all of which give you a choice of world-class wines and meals along with uninterrupted views of the valley. You can also enjoy a more thrilling experience by taking a tour of the valley via horseback at Cloud's End, or you can choose an adrenaline-pumped afternoon of paintball wars, quad biking or zip lining at Hermanus Forest Adventures. There are also hiking and mountain-biking trails on offer from other adventure businesses.

Left: A tree-lined dam at Hamilton Russell Vineyards evokes a sense of heavenliness.

Above: The mountain-biking routes in the Hemel-en-Aarde Valley take riders through breathtaking scenery.

This piece of paradise is an escape from the clamour of city life, and should be enjoyed at a leisurely pace. The valley offers a range of accommodation options, from self-catering cottages to elegant guest lodges on wine farms, all of which guarantee to give visitors a memorable experience.

In 1817, long before the 'grip of the grape' had seized the Hemel-en-Aarde Valley, Moravian missionaries, on the instruction of Lord Charles Somerset, founded a leper institute, locally known as the 'place of sorrow'. This isolated place began as a settlement of huts and vegetable gardens on land purchased by the government.

At first, the families of the lepers remained with their relatives, until Dr James Barry, the medical inspector for the colony, instructed that all the families had to leave. Dr Barry imposed strict policies and medical procedures at the leper colony, and also attempted to segregate the sexes to prevent the birth of children to the leper patients, but these rules proved almost impossible to enforce.

Dr Barry is famous for another reason – on her death, she was discovered to be a woman! At that time it was not permitted for a woman to study medicine or become a doctor.

Over 400 leper patients are buried in the Hemel-en-Aarde Valley. Although it is not known how the valley got its name, legend has it that the lepers, who were shunned and segregated in this remote place, where all they could see was the surrounding land and the sky above them, gave the valley its name. Others have suggested that it was derived from the writings of a nineteenth-century Moravian missionary, Brother Schmidt, who wrote:

'So high are the hills, which closely embrace the valley all around, that they seem to touch the sky and you cannot see anything but Heaven and Earth.'

In 1845, the government decided to move the leper colony to Robben Island. It was on this island that, decades later, Nelson Mandela would be incarcerated under the country's apartheid regime for most of his 27 years of political imprisonment.

Also steeped in the valley's history is the old Mission Station of the Moravian Church at Karwyderskraal, the 'transport rider's kraal'.

This land was once the homestead of a Scottish woman, Ella Gordon, known as quite an eccentric, who farmed here and trained her beloved horses to do tricks. Each time a horse died it was buried in her 'horse cemetery'. She undertook the building of a school and church on her farm where Moravian ministers held services. Ella died in 1958 at the age of 85 and is buried on the farm, which she bequeathed to the Moravian Church. Her home and the horse cemetery are still in existence, though in poor condition.

Camphill Farm Community was established in the valley in 1978. This farm, with its pastoral setting, is managed along biodynamic and organic principles oriented towards self-reliance and sustainability. The community school, based on Rudolf Steiner's method of teaching, offers quality education to both children and adults with special needs. Home industries on the farm include the production of organic vegetables, bread, dairy produce, herbs and candles. Central to the farm is its dairy herd from which the community benefits with fresh milk, butter, yoghurt and cheeses. The surplus products sold at local outlets help to fund the enterprise. The egg garden houses approximately 300 laying hens, which thrive on a natural diet. Foraging takes place on a rotational basis in four fields, managed according to a permaculture yard rotation system. A visit to Camphill gives insight into the wonderful way in which tending nature with care and respect creates a holistic cycle of life, energy and sustainability. Nowhere will you find a healthier, happier, better cared-for crowd of clucking chickens. A Camphill visit is inspirational!

The Camphill Farm Community was established in 1978 and provides residential care and meaningful work for adults with intellectual disabilities.

HERMANUS

Hemelrand, situated on the highest ridge of the Hemel-en-Aarde Valley, is a marvellous mountain farm that benefits from an exceptional terroir and a cool maritime influence. In addition to flourishing vineyards and the wines bottled here, this estate also cultivates several varieties of olives, including Leccino, Mission, Coratina and Frantoio. Hemelrand's scenic landscape of vineyards and olive groves melding with lavendar and rosemary fields is reminiscent of a Mediterranean vista.

Also located in the Hemel-en-Aarde Valley is the prestigious private estate, Bona Dea. *Liquidamber* trees line the road ascending to the deluxe complex set in the heart of a protea and orchid farm. In the evening, the trees are lit up with a galaxy of fairy lights, illuminating the estate and its extensive gardens and adding an enchanting dimension to the lavish out-of-the-ordinary ambience and tranquility of its surroundings. This exclusive function venue, which took first place in the Topvendor Wedding Awards in 2015, is set amid hectares of pristine fynbos and offers expansive views across the vineyards. Here passion for perfection is rivalled only by the celebration of elegance, beauty and joy.

The spiritual retreat, Volmoed, in the cradle of the valley, is watched over by the Sleeping Child Mountain. Bernhard and Jane Turkstra created this special place

Above and left: The Bona Dea Private Estate, at the beginning of the Hemel-en-Aarde Valley, is a luxurious wedding and conferencing destination.

Pages 178–179: De Bos Dam.

Set in its own tranquil valley, with a waterfall and a natural rock pool, Volmoed is a retreat and conference centre.

in 1986. Volmoed ('full of courage') is truly an inspirational place, and as close to heaven as one can get on earth. Above this sanctuary of breathtaking beauty, a chapel, embellished with stained-glass windows, stands beside a large lily pond, taking you far from the buzz of the town below.

The picturesque De Bos Dam in the valley is the main source of water for Hermanus. Long gone are the days when the springs could supply the villagers with all their water requirements. The first reservoir was built at the entrance of the town; its remains can still be seen today. In the early 1900s, three dams were built in the Mossel River. Later, a number of boreholes were drilled. As in many coastal areas, the surface water is brown because of the local vegetation. To avoid using this water, washing was done at the main springs where wash basins were built.

Construction of the dam began in 1976, where the Onrus River flows from its upper catchment area along the southern slopes of the Babylonstoren Mountains and the northern slopes of the Klein River Mountains, through two valleys – the upper Attaquas Valley and the lower Hemel-en-Aarde Valley. The river exits the Hemel-en-Aarde Valley between the Onrus Mountains and Olifantsberg, from where it enters the narrow coastal plain before finally flowing into the Onrus Lagoon, which opens into the Atlantic Ocean.

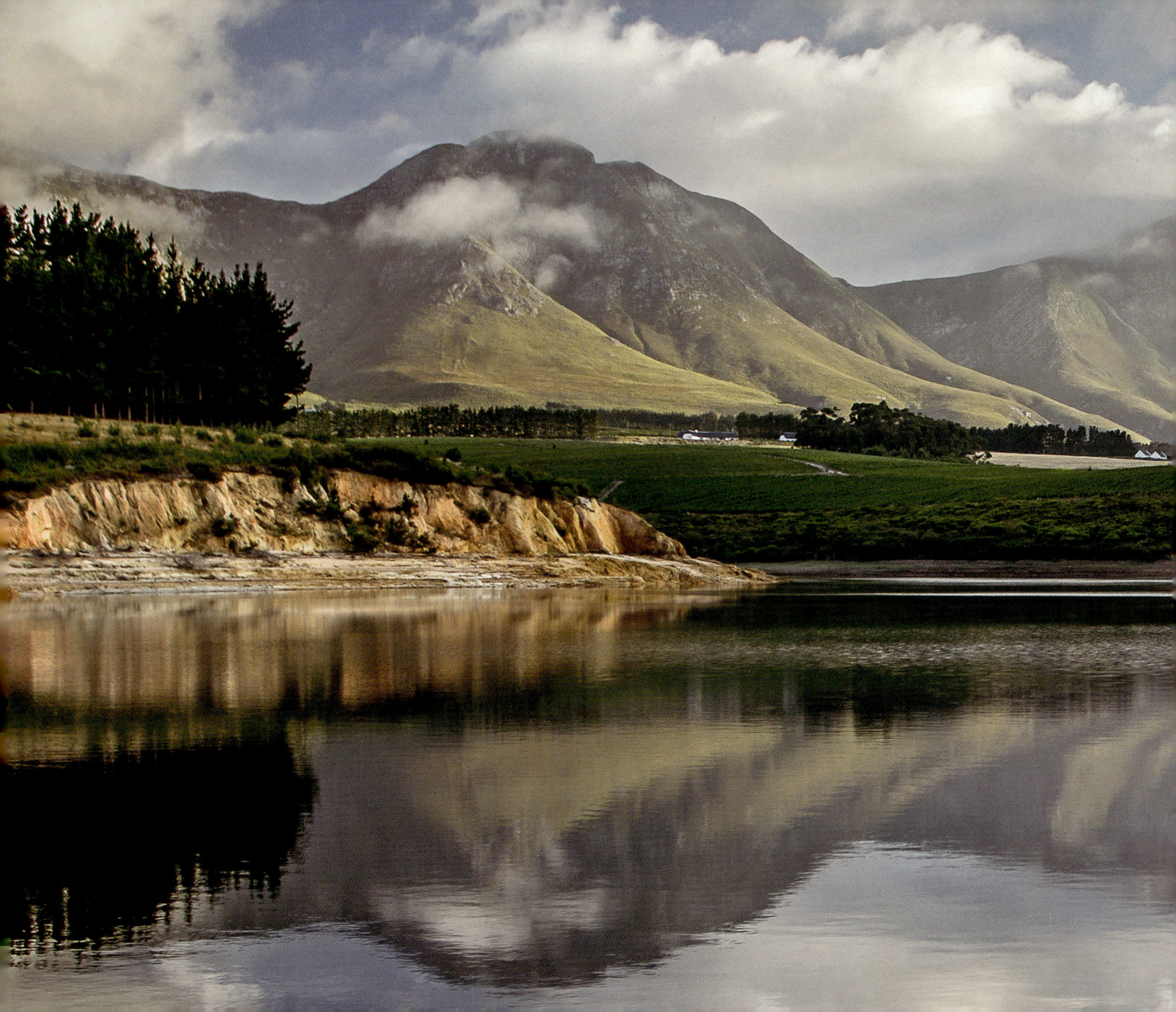

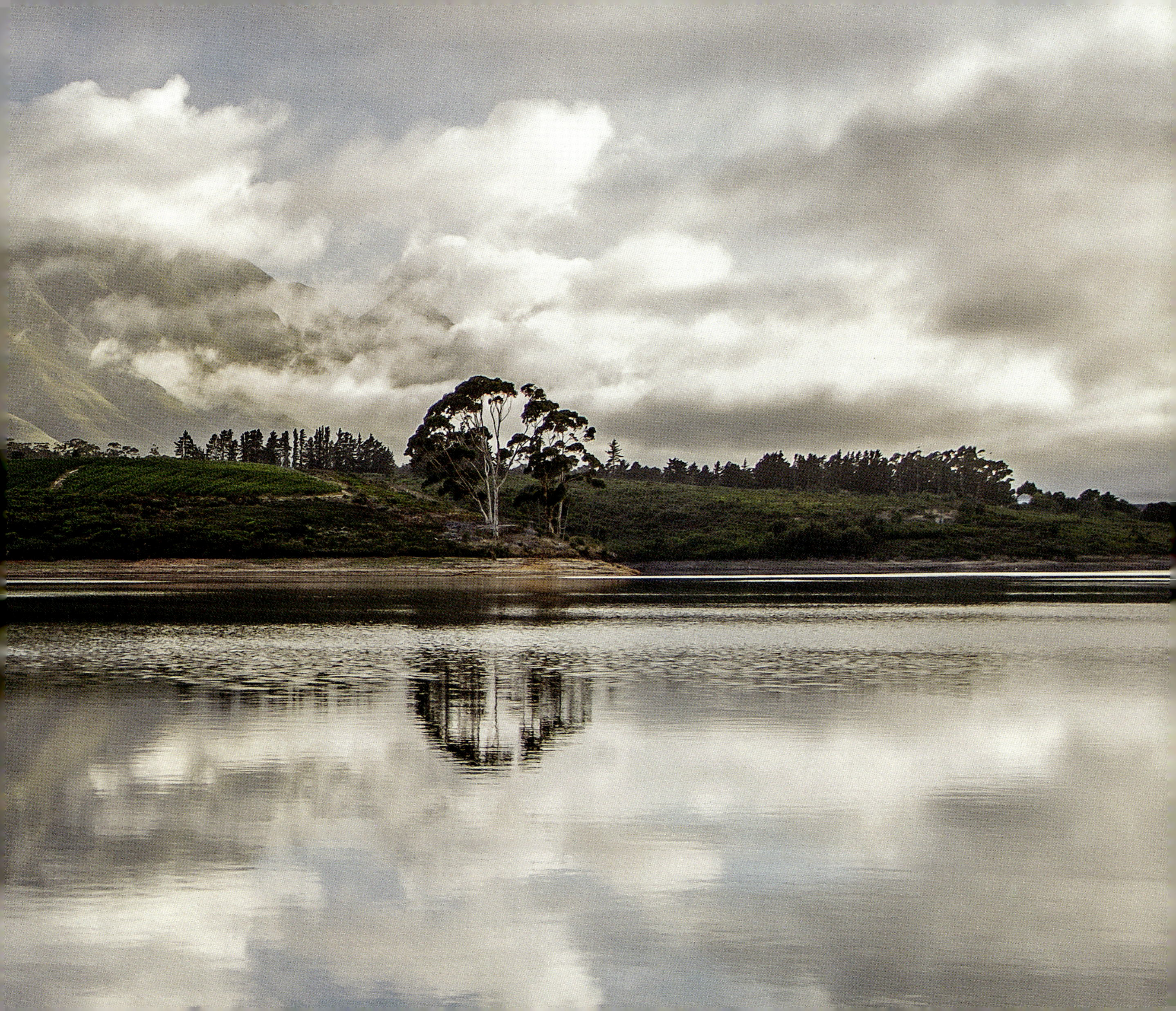

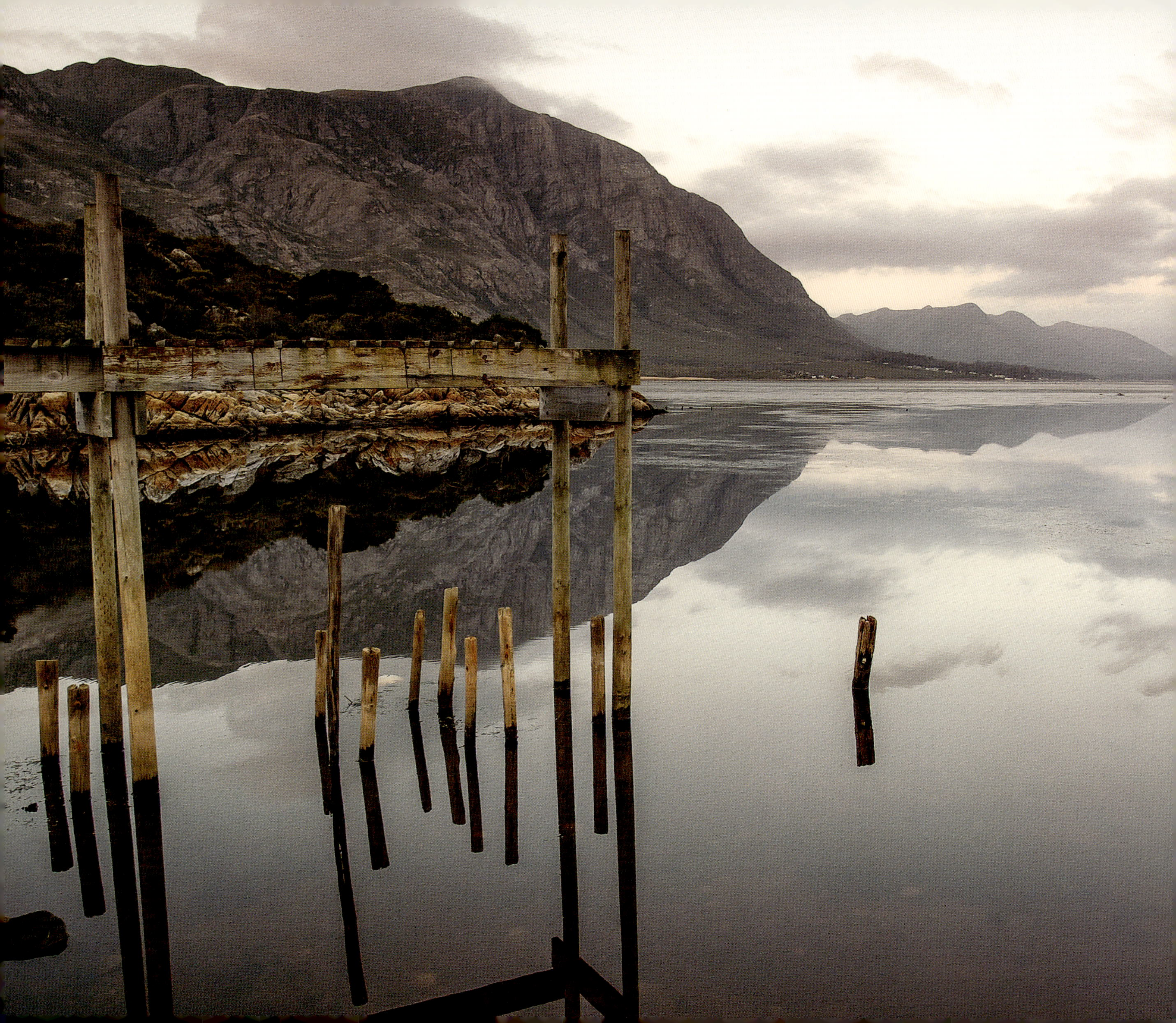

BEYOND HERMANUS

'I have learned that it is not the mountains that make destiny, but the grains of sand and the little pebbles.'

B. Traven

Klein River Lagoon

Where the Klein River Mouth meets the ocean, a sandbar created by the motion of the waves causes natural damming, forcing the river to spread into a large expanse of water.

This is the unique Klein River Lagoon, stretching from the village of Stanford to the sea. It is flanked on one side by mountain slopes and on the other by a 12-kilometre strip of sandy beach known as Die Plaat, which extends from the estuary of the lagoon to De Kelders. The tranquility of this protected eco-paradise makes it an ideal place for fishing, horse riding and long, peaceful walks.

The Hermanus Yacht Club, founded in 1950, is situated on the northern shores of the lagoon; although it is a private club, it welcomes day visitors. Boating and watersports enthusiasts gather here on weekends and during holiday seasons. One of the annual events is the Hermanus–Stanford canoe race that draws more than 100 competitors every year. The canoeists start at the Hermanus Yacht Club, creating an impressive picture of paddle power all the way to the finishing line at Stanford.

Since the development of residential buildings on the lagoon's shoreline, there has been continual controversy as to whether the waters flowing during the rainy season should be left to breach the sandbar or whether, as has often happened, the breach should be made with bulldozers, as a preventative measure against flooding. In either case, the opening of the lagoon mouth is an event not to be missed. Spectators can watch a trickle gradually grow into a torrent as the pent-up water follows its natural course to the sea.

Klein River Lagoon.

Much of the charm of Stanford lies in the well-preserved buildings that line its streets – from the Dutch Reformed Church (above) to the many quaint Victorian and Edwardian dwellings in the town centre (opposite).

Stanford

The road running east from Hermanus alongside the Klein River Lagoon takes you through a country setting of fynbos, agricultural land and vineyards before arriving, 25 kilometres later, at a quaint little village steeped in pioneering history. Stanford was established in 1857 on what was once the land of Sir Robert Stanford, owner of several farms in the Overberg region. He incurred the wrath of colonists when, in 1848, he provided produce to the *Neptune*, which carried convicts expelled to the Cape Colony. The colonists objected to them being settled in the Cape and refused to provide the ship with provisions. Stanford, still partially in the employ of the British army, was ordered by the government to provide the convicts with supplies. He was immediately labelled a traitor and ostracised by the colonists, which eventually led to his ruin.

Stanford village, with its Victorian-style houses so carefully preserved, exudes a charm reminiscent of a bygone era. In 1996 Stanford's infrastructure of original homesteads was declared an architectural conservation area.

The old-world charm of the village, with its market square and tree-lined streets, is enhanced by an eclectic mix of homes, shops and award-winning restaurants, while the quaint coffee shops, antique stores and art galleries that line the main road entice one to stop a while, slow down and enjoy the fresh country air.

Local places of interest to visit include, among others, the Birkenhead Brewery, the family-run Klein River Cheese on the Klein River Farmstead, Salmonsdam Nature Reserve, and the big cat reserve, Panthera Africa, which is a non-profit sanctuary for rescued big cats.

Hermanus histories

Stanford, established in 1857, is known for its well-preserved architecture, flowers and tranquility. Many of its buildings date back between 100 and 150 years. The market square in the centre of the village dates back to 1785. It is one of the few remaining market squares left undeveloped in South Africa.

Caledon Tourism, *Cape Overberg Meander 2004/5*

Once a rustic village off the beaten track, Stanford has become increasingly popular as a residential and holiday destination. Stanfordites include people from all walks of life who have made this naturalist's paradise their home.

Laina Lesicnik, a local resident and co-director of Stanford Players, which hosts an annual theatre production in the local church hall, and her husband, Erwin, chose to settle in the village some years ago. This is her story:

My husband and I were on a road trip through the Western Cape, looking for a new place to settle. Driving out of Hermanus towards Gansbaai, we passed the lagoon, lined with a dense forest of trees, which after a few kilometres gives way to rolling farmlands, grazing cows and frolicking horses. On the mountain slopes there are rambling farmhouses embellished with green vineyards. As we turned off the R43 into Stanford, we both knew we had come home.

There is a feeling here of easy, country living, with many children freely roaming the streets, skateboarding down the hills, and gathering in groups on the playgrounds. The sentiment 'it takes a village to raise a child' finds its expression here.

Stanford's communal village ethos extends to its country markets – Wednesdays at Graze Café, for freshly picked organic vegetables and healthy pressed juices, Saturday morning on the stoep of the Stanford Hotel, and the last Friday of each month the Sunset Market on the village green. Here the village community gathers to drink wine and break bread together, to shop for home-baked products and beautifully crafted items, and, most importantly, to catch up on all the local gossip.

The beautiful Klein River mountain range is an imposing, yet gentle presence in the village, one that pervades our awareness as we observe her ever-changing moods and hues.

Wandering down the picturesque lanes, you will eventually come across another hidden gem – the magical Klein River, which winds its way along the edge of the village. The river is a rich eco-habitat for over 200 species of bird, making Stanford a prime destination for birding enthusiasts. It is also home to turtles, otters, bass and other freshwater fish.

The river offers many other opportunities to enjoy nature and her pristine beauty – swimming, kayaking, or simply watching and listening to the birds that abound in the surrounding lush vegetation. Boating activities include river cruises on the *African Queen* and the *River Rat*.

The Stanford Wandelpad (Stanford Walking Trail) is a carefully maintained walking/running trail that follows the river as it gently meanders along its way; it is a favourite route for the town's many dog walkers and fitness seekers. Birders are in for a treat, too, as fish eagles, Cape eagle-owls and blue cranes can sometimes be seen.

The monthly Stanford Sunset Market takes place on the village green.

Stanford Wine Route

The Stanford Wine Route not only celebrates excellent wines of the Overberg, but each wine farm presents diverse enterprises and activities. The estates on the Stanford Wine Route include:

- Misty Mountains
- Sir Robert Stanford
- Stanford Hills
- Birkenhead Brewery and Walker Bay Estate
- Raka Wines
- Boschrivier Wines
- Brunia Wines
- Vaalvlei
- Springfontein

Most wine farms in this beautiful part of the countryside provide lunches and picnics to enjoy at your leisure in delightful tranquil settings.

Established in 2015, the Stanford Wine Route features prime estates such as Raka Wines (top right), Misty Mountains (above) and Sir Robert Stanford (right).

HERMANUS 185

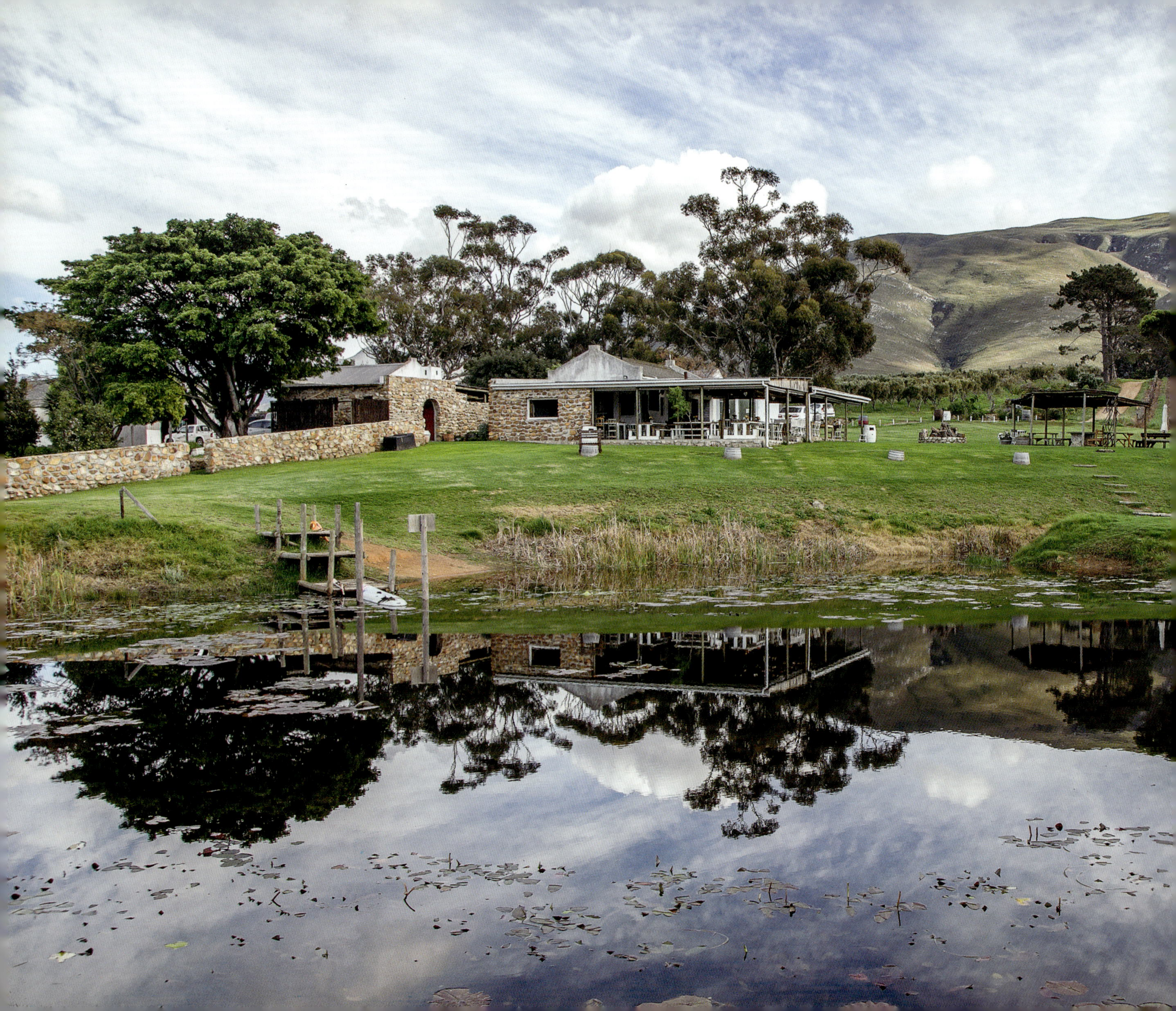

Photographer Johann Kruger was welcomed by the Stanford Wine Route and describes his experience as follows:

Apart from a world-class wine experience, the Stanford Wine Route is an invitation to kick off your shoes and let your hair down.

At Robert Stanford Estate a rather large pig followed me to the door of the wine-tasting room. With a heavy sigh and a grunt, it turned around. Unlike the pig, I received a warm welcome at every tasting room on the route.

A gentle stroll from the Robert Stanford tasting room will take you to the estate's Fynbos Distillery where liqueurs and grappa, as well as witblits, mampoer *and other exotic cocktails, are produced with equal parts of enthusiasm and fun. Prepare to spend some time here. The combination of adventurous flavours and a view over tranquil ponds will make this a tasting experience you will want to stretch out.*

For fine dining combined with farm hospitality, work your way to the estate's restaurant, The Royal Oke. But brace yourself, as you will have to fight off the geese.

Just a short drive further along, you will arrive at Stanford Hills. Enjoy beautifully presented fresh farm food and, of course, visit the tasting room to sample the estate's wines.

Kids of all ages can paddle on the pond here, or roam free on the vast lawns dotted with a jungle gym, sandpit and trampoline. Let them rediscover the lost art of self-entertainment.

A common thread linking all the estates along the route – from Raka Wines to Springfontein – is the personal touch derived from owner involvement. One senses that these farms, with their warm welcoming individual personalities, are the personal creative expressions of their stewards.

A beautifully renovated farm cottage, with sweeping views across the vineyards and dam, is the hub of The Tasting Room restaurant at Stanford Hills Estate.

Constructed along a fynbos-clad hill, the Grootbos Private Nature Reserve offers luxury and comfort in a pristine natural environment.

Grootbos Private Nature Reserve

Grootbos, with its stylish and innovative architecture, is a private nature reserve showcasing the flora and marine life at the southern tip of Africa. It is owned by the Lutzeyer brothers, Michael and Tertius, and consists of 2,500 hectares of coastal hillside. This five-star lodge is rated among the finest in the world, with beautifully appointed suites scattered along pathways fringed with fynbos and milkwood forests.

The Grootbos Foundation involves the local community in conservation initiatives and the sustainable harvesting of fynbos flowers. It also aims to improve economic and social conditions for workers by providing training, fair wages, health care and education. In 2016 the foundation was selected by *National Geographic* as one of 15 finalists in the World Legacy Awards.

Above and top: Grootbos's 2,500 hectares are home to more than 765 species of fynbos, four of which are endemic to the area.

The entrance to Klipgat Cave at De Kelders. Archaeological evidence shows that humans first inhabited this cave about 2,000 years ago.

De Kelders

The cliffs of De Kelders ('the cellars' or 'the caves'), 50 kilometres from Hermanus, also draw visitors to this coastline, especially during the whale season. The caves found here are the only freshwater caves on the African coast. Inside the caves is a pool, where the water is usually several degrees warmer than the sea. Excavations have revealed archaeological deposits from the Middle Stone Age (about 80,000 years ago), while more recent deposits point to Khoikhoi occupation of these caves approximately 2,000 years ago.

Gansbaai

Originally called Gansgat ('goose hole'), Gansbaai ('goose bay') was once, like Hermanus, a fishing paradise. The area became known soon after the legendary HMS *Birkenhead* ran aground here in 1852.

Situated along a remote craggy coastline, with spectacular cliffs, Gansbaai is surrounded by small bays, milkwood forests and fynbos nature reserves. Magnificent vistas from its cliffs stretch across Walker Bay to Hermanus and as far as Cape Point. A seven-kilometre scenic walk following the coastline from Gansbaai to De Kelders offers excellent viewing. With Dyer Island in close proximity, Gansbaai is rated as the great white shark capital of the world and is also a prime site for whale watching.

The lighthouse at Danger Point is a tourist attraction; you can climb the stairs to the revolving light and look out over the sea where the *Birkenhead* went down on her last voyage.

The African Penguin and Seabird Sanctuary (APSS) at Gansbaai is a rehabilitation centre for distressed seabirds and is also an educational platform informing the public of the marine work that is carried out by the facility.

Apart from its marine life, this region is home to over 200 species of indigenous fynbos. The annual Funky Fynbos Festival, held in September, celebrates this floral heritage.

In 2015 the Gansbaai Tourism Office won both the World Responsible Tourism Award and the African Responsible Tourism Award, with special reference to Grootbos Private Nature Reserve and Marine Dynamics.

Fishing boats set off daily from Gansbaai's small working harbour (above). Further along the coast is Danger Point Lighthouse (top).

The shipwreck of the HMS *Birkenhead*

At Gansbaai, Danger Point Lighthouse sweeps its beam across the sea where the famous HMS *Birkenhead* sank. This shipwreck has become legendary because of the courage shown by the troops on board.

At 18h00 on the evening of 25 February 1852, the HMS *Birkenhead*, under the command of Captain Robert Salmond, set out from Simon's Bay (Simon's Town) on its voyage to Algoa Bay and the Buffalo River Mouth on the eastern Cape coast. On board the iron-hulled paddle steamer, also rigged as a sailing vessel, were the ship's officers, its crew, several British Army regiments, and seven women and 13 children. The troops were bound for the Eighth Frontier War (1850–1853) on the eastern border of the Cape Colony.

It is not known what drew the ship so close to land, but in the early hours of the next morning it struck a rock lying below the surface of the sea, tearing the hull of the vessel open and drowning the men on the lower deck. Without time to say goodbye to their husbands and fathers, the women and children were hurried to the top deck and lowered to the water in a cutter.

Within a very short while the ship was sinking. Most of the men, including the captain, stood at their posts as the ship continued to go down. Some started clutching pieces of the wreckage as the ship rapidly descended to the seabed.

A schooner, the *Lioness*, picked up the women and children. Several men rowed ashore in a gig and were helped by the fishing folk of Harry's Bay. One of the survivors, the ship's doctor, Dr Culhane, borrowed a horse and rode at breakneck speed to Simon's Bay to alert the authorities to the tragedy. The HMS *Rhadamanthus* was immediately dispatched to see if there were any remaining survivors in the sea.

When the *Rhadamanthus* made contact with the *Lioness*, it was decided to tow her, with the survivors, back to Simon's Bay, as the wind had completely dropped by then. The HMS *Rhadamanthus* then returned to the scene of the wreck in search of more survivors. They found none.

When the HMS *Birkenhead* struck a rock along the coast near Danger Point in 1852, the soldiers on board were told to stand firm while the women and children were escorted into cutters and set out to sea.

Captain Salmond had advised the men to jump overboard and make for the boats as the ship sank, but instead they obeyed their military commanders' orders. It was Captain Wright and Lieutenant Girandot who instructed them to stand fast, anticipating that the boat with the women and children might be swamped.

Military discipline determined their tragic fate – but may have saved other lives – that night of the now famous *Birkenhead* disaster. This heroic deed set a precedent, and the 'Birkenhead Drill' of 'women and children first' has since become standard practice throughout the world.

Salvage experts located the sunken wreck of the *Birkenhead* in 1935. The last survivor, Hugh Todd, was one of the children saved; he died in Barkly East in the eastern Cape in 1937, at the age of 87.

To explore the mystery of this British troopship's final destiny, take a look at Nicholas Dekker's *Maqoma's Last War* and draw your own conclusions. Or read *Salvage of the Birkenhead,* a factual account by Allan Kayle of the professional diving crew who found the wreck and salvaged many of its artefacts and treasures.

Hermanus histories

The most famous *Birkenhead* story is of the chest of money that somehow arrived on the shore and was found by a local inhabitant, who became suddenly and inexplicably rich. Many things were washed up from wrecks along the wild and dangerous coasts around Danger Point, and disappeared before the customs officers could get there: bales of cloth, timber, barrels of oil or wine – and a chest of money would be a prize indeed.

Arderne Tredgold, *Village of the Sea – The Story of Hermanus*, 1965

Left and above: Of the estimated 643 people on board the *Birkenhead* when it sank, only 193 survived. It was only 43 years later, in 1895, that the Danger Point Lighthouse was built.

Cape cormorants, along with several other seabirds, are commonly seen at Dyer Island.

Dyer Island

Wilfred Chivell, skipper and owner of Dyer Island Cruises and Marine Dynamics, is an expert when it comes to the ecosystem and varied wildlife found on and around Dyer Island. Chivell, who has been a spear fisherman and wreck diver for over 20 years, grew up in the area. His ongoing relationship with conservation has set him up to work with top marine wildlife photographers as well as scientists specialising in whales, dolphins, seals and seabirds. His motto, he says, is to 'discover and protect'. Responsible tourism is his main objective, focusing on conservation, education, community upliftment and safety.

Operating from its base, The Great White House, at Kleinbaai, Dyer Island Cruises specialises in whale-watching and ecotours, while its sister company, Marine Dynamics, concentrates on shark viewing and shark cage diving. Both companies have been certified by Fair Trade in Tourism South Africa.

The companies operate throughout the year, except for the month of May. Between July and December excursions to the island are combined with boat-based whale watching. These cruises are on the *Whale Whisperer*, a specially designed boat with a large observation deck. Viewers are taken to what is possibly the only place in the world where both these travellers from Antarctica and great white sharks can be seen on the same trip.

Slashfin, a custom-designed aluminium boat, the first of its kind in the industry, takes shark spotters to Shark Alley, between Dyer Island and Geyser Rock – arguably the prime spot in the world for encountering great white sharks. The top deck of this luxury boat offers superb photographic opportunities, allowing for close-up footage. The best sightings occur in winter, between May and September.

Dyer Island Cruises and Marine Dynamics have received various awards for their business policies and conservation accomplishments. In November 2006, First Choice Responsible Tourism in London presented Dyer Island Cruises with the prestigious commendation for 'Best in Marine Environment'. Marine Dynamics was awarded the People's Choice Award in the 2016 African Responsible Tourism Awards.

Next to Dyer Island is Geyser Rock, where there is a colony of approximately 60,000 Cape fur seals.

BIBLIOGRAPHY

Ashton, Noel. 2015. *A Quick Guide to the Whales of Southern Africa.* Hermanus: Oceans of Africa.

Barnard, Lady Anne. 1910. *South Africa a Century Ago; Letters Written from the Cape of Good Hope (1797–1801).* London: Smith, Elder.

Best, Peter. 2003. *Whale Watching in South Africa: The Southern Right Whale.* Nedbank.

Blake, Rita. 1998. *Rooiels – A History and Other Stories.* Rooi-Els: Rooi-Els Ratepayers' Association.

Bruton, Mike. 1998. *The Essential Guide to Whales in Southern Africa.* Cape Town: David Philip, in association with the MTN Cape Whale Route.

Bulpin, T. V. 1970. *Discovering Southern Africa.* Cape Town: T. V. Bulpin Publications.

Burman, Jose. 1989. *Hermanus – A Guide to the Riviera of the South.* Cape Town: Human & Rousseau.

Burman, Jose. 1978. *Coastal Holiday – A Guide to South African Seaside Resorts.* Cape Town: Human & Rousseau.

Caledon Tourism. 2005. *Cape Overberg Meander 2004/5.*

Cockcroft, Vic and Joyce, Peter. 1998. *Whale Watch: A Guide to Whales and Other Marine Mammals of Southern Africa.* Cape Town: Struik.

Davie, Allan. 2008. *The Whale Trail: Southbound Pocket Guide.* Johannesburg: Southbound.

Dekker, Nicholas. 2005. *Maqoma's Last War.* Stanford: Cape Quest.

Diemont, Marius. 1978. The Iron Man of the Sea. *SA MAN*, May.

Du Toit, S. J. 2005. *The Overberg: Historical Anecdotes.* Paarl: S. J. du Toit.

Du Toit, S. J. 2002. *Hermanus Stories II: Historical Anecdotes of Hermanus.* Hermanus: S. J. du Toit.

Du Toit, S. J. 2001. *Hermanus Stories I: Historical Anecdotes of Hermanus.* Hermanus: S. J. du Toit.

Furst, Glenda. 2009. *Hermanus Cooks.* Hermanus: Self-published.

Gibson, Rex and Tyson, Harvey. 2007. *Hermanus Golf Club Centenary Album 1907–2007.* Hermanus: Hermanus Golf Club.

Giliomee, Herman. 2003. *The Afrikaners: Biography of a People.* Cape Town: Tafelberg.

Gilpin, Daniel. 2006. *The Mighty Oceans:* Reader's Digest.

Gould, Larry. 2013. *The Hermanus Golf Club.* Accessed March 2017 from http://www.larrygouldgolf.com.

Green, Lawrence. 1975. *Grow Lovely, Growing Old.* Cape Town: Howard Timmins.

Heard, Duncan. 2016. The Vermont Salt Pan. *The Village News,* April.

Hermanus Info. 2005. *Hermanus.* Hermanus: Overberg Media.

Jensen, Albert. 1979. *Wildlife of the Oceans.* New York: Harry N. Abrams, Inc.

Kayle, Allan. 1990. *Salvage of the Birkenhead.* Johannesburg: Southern Book Publishers.

Kotze, Pieter. 2005. The Earth's Varying Magnetic Fields. *Village Life,* February/March, No. 10.

Kruger, Bernhard. 1966. *The Pear Tree Blossoms – The History of the Moravian Church in South Africa 1737–1869.* Doctoral thesis, Rhodes University, Grahamstown.

Lloyd, Frieda. 2015/2016. Guide to the Hermanus Wine Route R320. *The Village News,* December/January.

Luyt, Berdine. 2014. *In Those Days – The Story of Joey Luyt and the Marine Hotel.* Edited by Robin Lee. Hermanus: Hermanus History Society.

McCann, Gerald. 2012. *The History of Bot Rivier and the Old Cape Wagon Way.* Digital Print Solution.

Mouton, Mare. 2005. They Make Sure It is True North. *Village Life,* February/March, No. 10.

Overberg Info 2003/04. Hermanus: Overberg Media.

Steyn, de Waal. 2016. Great White Numbers Are Dwindling. *The Village News,* July.

Tredgold, Arderne. 1965. *Village of the Sea – The Story of Hermanus.* Cape Town: Human & Rousseau.

Van der Ross, Richard. 2005. *Up From Slavery: Slaves at the Cape: Their Origins, Treatment and Contribution.* Cape Town: Ampersand Press.

Van Zyl, Philip (Editor). 2016. *Platter's 2016 South African Wine Guide.* Hermanus: John Platter SA Wineguide (Pty) Ltd.

Van Zyl, Philip (Editor). 2014. *Platter's 2014 South African Wine Guide.* Hermanus: John Platter SA Wineguide (Pty) Ltd.

ACKNOWLEDGEMENTS

BETH HUNT

I was motivated to rewrite this coffee-table book on Hermanus by requests from visitors to my bookshop, Hemingways of Harbour Road, for an updated guide to this fast-growing town of the Overberg. A fortuitous meeting with photographer Johann Kruger at his Cinema Café led to a creative collaboration with Johann and his brother, Kobus, of Action Photoz. This has been a marvellous and exciting project. As always, my thanks go to my husband, Noel, for his encouragement. My great appreciation also goes to Pippa Parker and her team at Penguin Random House who have helped to transform the idea of *Hermanus* into reality.

JOHANN KRUGER

The following close friends were bribed and trapped into becoming the beautiful 'face' of the people of Hermanus: Neethling Naude, Tawani Naude, Stefan and Marene Pieterse, the Krynauw family, Elizma du Toit, Marius van der Westhuizen, Allen and Michelle Pass, Anthea van der Pluym, Danie and Lize Steyn, and the De Graeve family (including Neo and Nell).

Bevan Pope, you really rose to the occasion. Your appreciation and enthusiasm for your home town is unparalleled, as is your excitement about paragliding.

Zané Joubert, you made the Romantiques shoot come alive. Thank you for a fun, time-travelling photo shoot.

Kobus is my brother in life and in photography. My earliest memory of us practising photography together is of me throwing rocks at hippos, because Kobus wanted the classic open-mouth hippo shot against the sunset. We still push the limits when we work together!

Thank you Beth Hunt for inviting us on this creative journey. Your dedication to research and creative writing was an inspiration to us as photographers. Most of all, thank you for the hours of making facts fun with alliteration!

On another note, thanks to Pippa Parker from Penguin Random House; it is truly an honour for this book to have been selected by you.

A very special note of thanks goes to my parents, who kept the business afloat during many, many hours of photographic excursions. It's the kind of favour only parents would do. Thank you for your very practical faith and support.

KOBUS KRUGER

I am grateful for the various talents God has bestowed upon me, though photography is the most fun and satisfying one.

Thank you Beth and Johann for taking me along on this awesome adventure. And thanks, too, for the fun, inspirational progress meetings … your creativity knows no bounds.

Janina, my rock star of a wife, provided support whenever it was required, whether it was taking care of me, managing the household, or providing level-headed input when it seemed as if I was losing perspective. Thank you.

I also want to give thanks to my parents. It's always a comfort to know they are in my corner, rooting for me, no matter what.

To Pippa Parker, thanks for finding room for this publication in an already full schedule. Calling Penguin Random House our 'home' is a dream come true, something many can only dream about.

Lastly, to the many people who made it possible for Johann and me to create the images that fill these pages, thank you.

Author Beth Hunt with photographers Johann Kruger (left) and Kobus Kruger (right).

Dawn over the New Harbour.